Christ the Center of Biblical Time

Christ the Center of Biblical Time

The Unity and Logic of the Bible's Story

Andrew Messmer

RESOURCE *Publications* · Eugene, Oregon

CHRIST THE CENTER OF BIBLICAL TIME
The Unity and Logic of the Bible's Story

Resource Publications
An Imprint of Wipf and Stock Publishers
199 W. 8th Ave., Suite 3
Eugene, OR 97401

www.wipfandstock.com

PAPERBACK ISBN: 979-8-3852-7949-4
HARDCOVER ISBN: 979-8-3852-7950-0
EBOOK ISBN: 979-8-3852-7951-7

VERSION NUMBER 04/10/26

All quotations come from the English Standard Version (ESV).

Dedication

To my wife, my faithful companion, who patiently listened to me talk about this book for many years.

To Warren Gage, who taught me to read Scripture in a new way.

Contents

List of Illustrations and Tables

Preface

THIS BOOK BEGAN IN 2015 when I began reflecting, in a new way, on the Old Testament story and how it organically finds its fulfillment in Jesus Christ. Before that time, of course I was acquainted with other well-known systems of biblical interpretation, but for all the help they offered —and they did offer much help— they still left me wanting more, especially with respect to the unity, logic, and development of the Old Testament story. My longings were satisfied when I read two works published by Oscar Cullmann and Warren Gage which had the extraordinary quality of explaining simply, yet elegantly and convincingly, different aspects of the logical development of the Old Testament storyline and its fulfillment in Jesus Christ.[1] Their works were written independently of each other and with different ends in view, but I hope to show that they can be read together such that the result is an even deeper, more satisfactory reading of the Scriptures. The purpose of this book is to do just that: to combine and develop the insights of Oscar Cullmann and Warren Gage, and to present a unified reading of the biblical story. This is not to suggest that this new reading of the

1. I have read Gage's book very closely at least five times (feeling physically fatigued after each completion), and I also had the immense privilege of spending a few days with him in Spain in March, 2019, during which time we devoted several hours to discussing the ideas laid out in his book.

Bible is the only legitimate one, but rather that it offers yet another fruitful way of doing so.

In the Introduction, I offer a summary of the pertinent arguments of Cullmann's and Gage's works. This will be foundational for the rest of the work, and readers not already familiar with their work should pay close attention to its contents. Chapters one through eight contain the primary contribution of this book, which is my attempt to offer a "Cullmannian–Gageian" reading of the biblical story, which may be described as a chiastic–cyclical reading which begins with Adam, centers on Christ, and ends with all of humanity. Finally, some appendices have been included to provide additional information that lies slightly afield the book's primary focus.

This book is not written for professional academics —although I think that they will be challenged by its contents and rewarded for their careful study—, but for pastors, students, and informed laymen who seek to know the unity and development of the biblical story from start to finish. In order to facilitate comprehension, I have avoided extensive footnotes and placed at the beginning of the chapters the primary biblical texts for each cycle and stage. Special vocabulary that is used in Scripture at key points is written with inverse commas (""), and an appendix provides the Hebrew equivalents for those interested.[2]

2. The vocabulary applies only to the Hebrew words used in OT; no vocabulary has been included for the Greek words used in the NT which may or may not be derived from the OT.

Acknowledgements

I WOULD LIKE TO THANK Warren Gage, for his interaction with me on the overall idea of this work: if it were not for him and his writing ministry, this book would not exist. I would like to thank the members at Calvary Church (Plainfield, IN) who prayed for me while I was in the last stages of writing and interacted with me as I taught it during Sunday school and shared it during informal conversations. I would like to thank Nick and the Interlibrary loan staff at the Plainfield Public Library for always getting books and articles for me in a timely manner.

List of Abbreviations

AH	*Against Heresies*
ANE	Ancient Near East
Antiq.	*The Antiquities of the Jews*
ARN	*Avot de Rabbi Nathan*
BT	*The Bible Translator*
EB	*Estudios bíblicos*
EJT	*European Journal of Theology*
HUCA	*Hebrew Union College Annual*
JBL	*Journal of Biblical Literature*
JSOT	*Journal for the Study of the Old Testament*
LXX	Septuagint
MT	Masoretic Text
Ps. Sol.	*Psalms of Solomon*
RTS	*The Reformed Theological Review*
SBJT	*Southern Baptist Journal of Theology*
VT	*Vetus Testamentum*
WST	*Warszawskie Studia Teologiczne*
WTJ	*Westminster Theological Journal*
ZAW	*Zeitschrift für die alttestamentliche Wissenschaft*

Introduction: Bringing Together Two Great Ideas

Oscar Cullmann and Warren Gage: Two Great Ideas[1]

IN HIS BOOK *CHRIST AND TIME*, Oscar Cullmann argued that God's plan of redemption involved the "election of a minority for the redemption of the whole" which he called the "principle of representation." His idea was that God uses representative mediators —such as a chosen individual or group of people— through whom he blesses the rest of creation. He combined this principle with another which he called "progressive reduction." By this he meant that as each chosen individual or group of people fail in their representative mediatorial roles, God elects new mediators who represented progressively smaller spheres of humanity. These two principles provided Cullmann with the logic needed to understand the development of the Old Testament and its trajectory into the New. The overall structure of representation and progressive reduction that Cullmann discerned had four stages: from mankind as a whole (summed up in Adam), to one nation (Israel), to a remnant (those of whom the prophets speak), to one man (Jesus Christ).

From here, with Christ seen as the great turning point in the biblical storyline, Cullmann argued that progressive reduction

1. Cullmann, *Christ and Time*, 115–17; Gage, *The Gospel of Genesis*.

changed to "progressive advance." By this, he meant that the reduction seen throughout the Old Testament was reversed after Christ, such that God began to work through more and more people to bless the rest of creation. We could visualize his basic idea in the following chiasm:

This reading of the Old Testament story opened up the logic of God's election with regard to both time and people: as time advanced from Adam onward, God worked with a smaller group of representatives through whom he sought to bless the whole of creation. At the same time, this reading forces the issue regarding the necessary fulfillment of the Old Testament story in Jesus Christ: sooner or later the principle of reduction would come to center on just one man, and the fate of humanity would rest squarely on his shoulders. It is as if the entire Old Testament had closed with this question: Could it be that God will find just one man who will be faithful to his covenant, through whom he will be able to bless all creation? Thus, according to this reading, Jesus came at exactly the right moment, or as Paul said, in the fullness of time (Gal 4:4; cf. Rom 5:6; 1 Tim 2:6; Tit 1:3). The key idea to take away from Cullmann is that the biblical story is a giant chiasm of progressive reduction that turns into progressive advance after the coming of Christ.

In his book *The Gospel of Genesis*, Warren Gage argued that Genesis 1–7 was a macrocosmic paradigm that foreshadowed the microcosmic paradigm of Israel, specifically with regard to her two temple periods. The fact that the world was covered in the waters of chaos in Genesis 1:2 and again in Genesis 7 implies that the opening chapters of Genesis formed a complete cycle from creation to (re)creation. Gage argued that the paradigm consists of five progressive stages: creation, man, fall, division, and judgment. By this, Gage meant that: God created in Genesis 1, he chose a man and made a covenant with him in Genesis 2, the man sinned in Genesis 3, his seed was divided and placed in conflict in Genesis 4–5, and God judged the wickedness of man in Genesis 6–7.[2] We could visualize his basic idea in the following graphic:

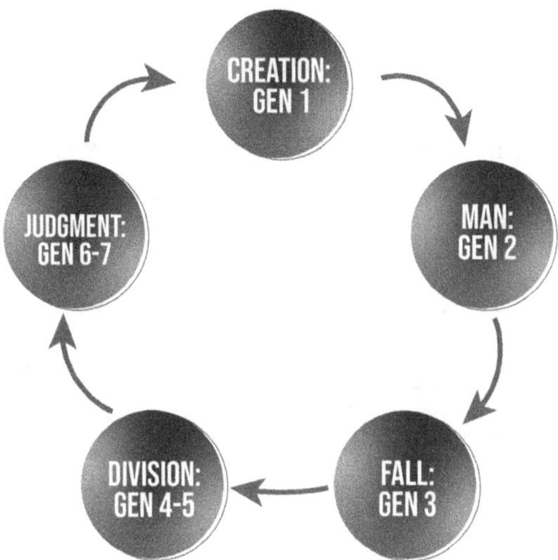

This reading of the Old Testament story is immensely valuable since it lays the groundwork for identifying similar cycles in the rest of Scripture and even makes it possible to predict the development of the cycle(s) along the lines of creation, man, fall, division,

2. He also argued that the cycle of Gen 1–7 corresponded to another macrocosmic paradigm, beginning with Noah and ending at the return of Christ, when another flood-like destruction of the earth will take place. For NT and other early Christian support, cf. Matt 24:37–39 *pars*; 2 Pet 3:5–7; *Barn.* 6:13.

and judgment.[3] The key idea to take away from Gage is that Genesis 1–7 contains a cycle that becomes a paradigm for interpreting subsequent cycles throughout Scripture.

Cullman and Gage: Developing their Ideas

Having summarized Cullman's and Gage's key ideas, I will now show how they can be combined and developed.[4] While Cullmann was correct in discerning the principles of representation and progressive reduction as crucial to interpreting God's workings with humanity, he only argued for four cycles in the biblical story. However, strong evidence suggests that seven major cycles are found in the Old Testament story, resulting in a progressive reduction that carries the story from beginning to end in a downward spiral that hinges on Jesus Christ, who then initiates the age of progressive advance. Extended discussion of these cycles is found in the subsequent chapters, but they may be outlined briefly as follows:

1. From Adam, representing all mankind
2. to Noah, representing half of mankind (Seth's line)
3. to Abraham, representing one nation of mankind (Eber's line)
4. to Moses, representing the physical chosen descendants of Abraham (Jacob's line)
5. to Joshua, representing the spiritual chosen descendants of Abraham (Jacob's line)
6. to David, representing one tribe of Israel (Judah)

3. Bruce Waltke has endorsed Gage's general thesis (*Old Testament Theology*, 292–302). Another way to divide the cycles would be along the lines presented in Judg 2:6–19 and Neh 9:26–31, which can be generalized as obedience, disobedience, oppression, repentance, and deliverance (cf. Trompf, "Notions of Historical Recurrence," 219–25).

4. For a brief statement of some important aspects that are explained in further detail throughout my work, cf. Wright, *The New Testament and the People of God*, 216. Reading Israelite history as consisting of cycles is ancient, as illustrated by *Mid. Ps.* 118:22 (on Ps 118:24), which speaks of enslavement following every redemption.

7. to Zerubbabel, representing the remnant of one tribe (exiles)
8. to one man, Jesus Christ, representing all mankind.[5]

Thus, this more complete series of downward cycles could be depicted in the following partial chiasm:[6]

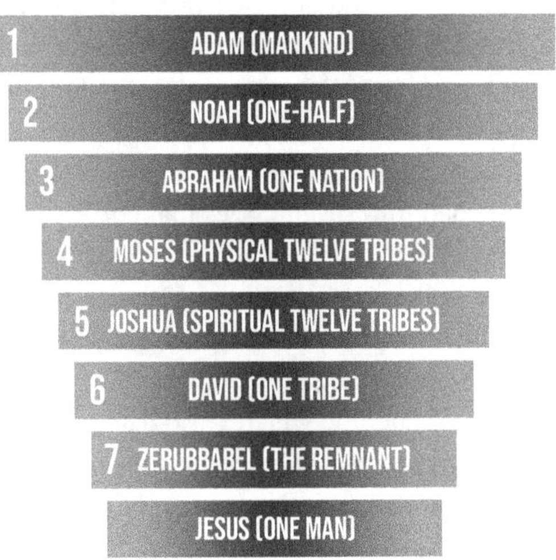

Although not mentioned by Cullmann, in addition to the progressive reduction of humanity, a progressive reduction of land is also apparent: Adam was given the whole world; Noah's descendants were split-up into three major groups, which were then further divided into seventy nations; Abraham was promised territory between the Nile and Euphrates rivers; Moses never led God's people into the Promised Land and Joshua's conquest was incomplete; David's and Solomon's kingdoms only briefly controlled the territory between the Nile and Euphrates rivers, and their descendants old ruled over the southern kingdom; and Zerubbabel and the exiled community were limited to Jerusalem

5. Regarding the first three cycles, Bruce Waltke gestures toward many of the same ideas presented here, but ultimately takes them in a different direction (*Old Testament Theology*, 305–11).

6. For the full chiasm, see chapter 8 below.

and its surrounding environs. By the time Jesus arrives, the hopes of humanity will be placed in one human body.

Cullmann was right to notice that the Book of Acts portrays a reversal of the Old Testament story: when Christ told his disciples that they would be his witnesses "in Jerusalem, and in all Judea and Samaria, and to the end of the earth" (Acts 1:8), this not only foreshadows the basic contours of the book of Acts but also generally mirrors the inverse of the Old Testament story. Just as there was a progressive reduction in the Old Testament, there is a progressive advance in the book of Acts. I am not arguing that Luke's book can be divided into seven cycles that correspond exactly to the seven cycles in the Old Testament, and my primary interest throughout this work resides in the progressive reduction in the Old Testament, but at a general level, Cullmann seems justified in arguing that the Book of Acts functions to reverse the Old Testament's progressive reduction, which I also defend here.

While Gage was correct in discerning a cycle of five stages in Genesis 1–7 and that this cycle was repeated throughout the biblical story, his work focused on the relationship between Genesis 1–7 (macrocosm) and Israel (microcosm) and did not explore all the cycles found throughout the Old Testament. Thus, his vision was more limited than the one presented here, and while I will not attempt to negate his insights, I do wish to develop them.[7]

As stated above, strong evidence suggests that there are seven cycles in the Old Testament, with Jesus Christ functioning as the climactic eighth cycle, similar to the beginning of a new week and "eighth day" theology. The biblical cycles do not begin with just a few important biblical figures such as Adam, Noah, and David, but rather with arguably every major one: Adam, Noah, Abraham and the patriarchs, Moses, Joshua, David (and Solomon),

7. Gage discussed one full cycle that spanned Gen 1–7, and four nearly complete cycles that spanned Gen 8–12, Israel's two temple periods, and Jesus. He did not discuss judgment for any of these latter cycles because he saw them as still future (*Gospel of Genesis*, 14–15). However, at times he made passing comments that contribute to the main thesis that I advance here (e.g., *Gospel of Genesis*, 28–29). Many of my observations regarding these cycles are taken from his work.

and Zerubbabel. They all find their fulfillment, of course, in Jesus Christ, in whom all God's promises are yes and amen (2 Cor 1:20).

One of the great strengths of the paradigm I am presenting here is that it has not been artificially imposed onto the biblical story, but rather arises from a careful reading of Scripture itself.[8] In fact, several scholars have argued for very similar interpretations of Old Testament texts to the ones I am arguing for here, but they have done so on a more limited scale.[9] Many scholars take for granted that Genesis 1–7 forms a unit from creation to re-creation, and it is becoming more common to see that the Noah story is a recapitulation of the Adam story, meaning that Genesis 1–11 presents us with two cycles which parallel each other.[10] From there, since antiquity it has been recognized that Abraham functions as a kind of new Adam,[11] and many scholars recognize the Exodus as a kind of new creation as well,[12] which itself suggests that between Abraham and Moses, there is at least some kind of cycle that has been completed. After the Exodus, fewer cycles have been recognized by other scholars, although many have recognized that themes such as new creation, new Adam, exile, and exodus continue to repeat throughout Scripture.[13] What I attempt to do in this book is to combine and organize all these insights, fill in

8. The weakness of artificially imposed paradigms, present in so many methodologies of OT theology, was pointed out by Hasel, *Old Testament Theology*, 28–114.

9. John Sailhamer gestures toward a similar reading with his term "narrative typology." Although his comments were focused on the Pentateuch, they can be applied to the broader biblical corpus: "Earlier events foreshadow and anticipate later events. Later events are written to remind the reader of past narratives" (*Pentateuch as Narrative*, 37).

10. For example, Sasson, "The 'Tower of Babel,'" 211–19; Rendsburg, *The Redaction of Genesis*, 7–25; Wright, *The New Testament and the People of God*, 216; Morales, *Exodus Old and New*, 13–14.

11. For example, *Gen. Rab.* 14.6.

12. For example, Athas, "The Creation of Israel," 30–59 (esp. 51–57); Morales, *Exodus Old and New*, 7–103.

13. For example, Roberts and Wilson, *Echoes of Exodus*.

the holes, demonstrate the logic and consistency of the cycles and their stages, and show how Christ fulfills it all.[14]

The issue of correctly identifying cycles, stages, and themes is an important one, and I have employed two basic principles in doing so. First, I have paid close attention to linguistic parallels. The creation and exodus cycles are the most formative for the others, and thus when their vocabulary is used elsewhere, I understand it to be significant. For example, the same vocabulary as Eve's "seeing," "desiring," and "taking" the fruit of the tree of the knowledge of good and evil is used in other cycles to recount the fall stage, and I understand the similar vocabulary was meant to evoke the original fall in the garden of Eden. Second, I have paid close attention to thematic parallels. This second principle recognizes that the Bible uses rich imagery which varies in the way it describes different events, and thus exact linguistic precision should not always be expected. Thematic parallels should not be seen as inferior to linguistic ones, but rather as complementary. An example of a thematic parallel would be the idea of a flood: God used a flood of water to judge the wicked earth in Genesis 6–7, but a flood of invading armies to judge his wicked people and send them into exile (e.g., Ps 124:1–5).

Each cycle corresponds to a major turning point in the biblical narrative: creation, flood, promise, Exodus, conquest, kingship, exile and return, and Jesus Christ. Also, each turning point has its respective covenant, or at least an affirmation of a previous one: Adamic, Noahic, Abrahamic, Mosaic, Davidic, New,

14. Some may accuse this approach of eisegesis, but a good case can be made, not only for a typological reading of the OT text, but also for a typological writing of the OT text; e.g., Link Jr. and Emerson, "Searching for the Second Adam." Although offering a somewhat different approach than the one I am offering here, the comments of G. W. Trompf are insightful (speaking of Josh–2 Kgs): "The main point is, however, that the writer bequeathed an account of about six centuries in which history, in a special sense, repeated itself. His picture of the repeated acts of transgression against God's commandments, and the repeated consequences of such disobedience, his characterization of recurrent 'event-shapes'—typical transgressions, typical warnings, fitting deaths and recompenses—all reflect a preoccupation with historical recurrence" ("Notions of Historical Recurrence," 223).

and fulfillment in Jesus. As will be demonstrated in subsequent chapters, once one knows how to identify the various stages of the cycles, a predictable pattern emerges such that the cycles become easily identifiable and practically suggest themselves. If we were to return to the visual depiction of Gage's cycle, the only modification necessary would be to reproduce it seven times, and to interlock the cycles in a downward spiral such that one cycle's end is the next cycle's beginning, which is smaller, both numerically and geographically, than the previous one.

Reading the Old Testament story in this way makes it clear that it is driving toward the one man, Jesus Christ, who is quite literally the last hope for mankind. He initiates the final cycle, never again to be advanced or bettered in any way. He is the fulfillment of the paradigm that Gage correctly discerned in his work and initiates the progressive advance that Cullmann rightfully noted in his, which reversed the progressive reduction found throughout the Old Testament and opened God's original plan of representative mediatorship to all mankind. Cullmann was right to argue that all history forms a chiastic structure which centers on Jesus Christ: God's election of mankind is reduced progressively until the entire weight of the Old Testament rests squarely on the shoulders of one man, Jesus Christ, and then progressively opens in chiastic fashion to include all humanity once more. There is a certain aesthetic beauty to this way of reading the biblical story that is difficult to resist.

Understanding history to be cyclical was a common idea in antiquity.[15] There were some variations of the idea —such as whether the cycle was universal or more localized— but the idea was basically the same: history repeats itself. In this way, Scripture fits in quite well with ancient understandings of history. However, the biblical story is not recounting several variations of an endlessly repeating cycle, but rather uses the cycles to form a progressive

15. Cf. Trompf, *The Idea of Historical Recurrence*. My reading of the OT finds some parallels with several ancient divisions of history into four/five ages of man, in that there is a repeating cycle that worsens with each renewal (e.g., Hesiod, *Works and Days*; Ovid, *Metamorphoses*).

downward spiral that has a purpose: to draw all biblical history into a decisive point that will be decided by one man, Jesus Christ.

As will be seen throughout my work, in addition to developing the independent insights of Cullmann and Gage, I have carefully noted how each of Gage's five stages contains several themes. The creation stage contains themes such as creation from chaos, creation battle,[16] God's Spirit, God's word, temple, and rest. The man stage contains themes such as election, the concept of being formed outside and brought in ("going forth"), a mixed multitude, a mountain and garden (often featuring a river and tree), and divine blessing and commands. The fall stage contains themes such as a lack of vigilance, a woman who is deceived and/or seduced, usurpation, knowledge of sin (and its subsequent actions such as shame, hiding, and clothing), curse, and forgiveness. The division stage contains themes such as division between the seeds, persecution, rival cities, apostasy and intermarriage,[17] prophets/preachers of righteousness, and affliction/crying out. The judgment stage contains themes such as chaos and flood, exile and expulsion, and the deliverance of a righteous remnant.

A summary of each cycle would take the following shape (with key words and concepts in italics): God's plan has been to *create* and defeat *chaos* by his *word* and *Spirit* and establish a *temple* in which he *rests*, and to *choose a man* whom he has *formed outside* and *brought forth* into a *garden* on a *mountain*, where he will give him a *divine blessing and commands*. However, due to man's *lack of vigilance*, he is *deceived* and sins, usually connected with a *woman* or general *deception*, and thus his right to rule is *usurped*. Man becomes *aware of his sin*, after which God *curses* him, but also offers him *forgiveness*. Subsequent generations are *divided*, with the ungodly line *persecuting* the godly one and establishing *cities* of self-rule. Through *apostasy* and *inter-marriage*, the godly line slowly loses its distinctiveness, despite the warnings of

16. In academic literature, this often referred to by its German name, *Schöpfungskampf*.

17. The close connection between spiritual and sexual immorality will become clear throughout this work.

prophets and *preachers of righteousness*. The godly line is *afflicted* and *cries out* to God for deliverance. God then *judges* and *exiles* those responsible and brings *chaos* back on the order he had established. Nevertheless, he *delivers a righteous remnant* and uses them to begin the subsequent cycle.[18]

Readers should know that while I am not claiming to provide all the real and imagined parallels between the stages of the various cycles, I am attempting to provide all the important ones which are shared not merely between a few cycles (e.g., only between the Adam and Moses cycles), but between most or all of them. Additionally, readers should be alerted to the fact that Scripture provides several mini-cycles and echoes of stages and themes that are not presented here. For example, the story of King Uzziah echoes the fall stage, and the story of Sodom and Gomorrah echoes the judgment stage, but neither have been included since they do not form part of a complete cycle from creation to judgment, nor do they fit into the universal story of progressive reduction. However, for those interested in seeing the parallels, they can be found in Appendix III.

In the following chapters, the cycles are presented in chronological order and divided into their various stages. Regarding dominant motifs, Genesis 1–7 and the Exodus event provide the basic features and concepts for the other themes, and thus most cycles will be compared to these.[19]

18. Not every theme will be found in every stage and cycle, but each cycle has features of each of the five stages and many of the themes appear as well. G. W. Trompf similarly writes (speaking about the Greco-Roman tradition): "belief in cyclical recurrence is not equivalent to belief in exact or even near-exact repetition" (*The Idea of Historical Recurrence*, 84). This is true for the biblical context as well, as will be shown throughout the work. Many modern-day westerners prefer uniformity of language and explicit statements whereas many other cultures —including those in which Scripture was written— are more open to diversity of language and implicit allusions.

19. Genesis 1–7 is the basic cycle, and the Exodus arguably is the foundational creation story for the people of Israel. Gage states insightfully, "The inscripturation of the creation account was *ex eventu* from the perspective of the Red Sea, so the Mosaic record of creation is chronologically but not logically precedent to the record of redemption from Egypt" (*Gospel of Genesis*, 20 n. 14).

Chapter 1: Adam, Representing All Mankind

Genesis 1–7

THIS IS THE FOUNDATIONAL cycle for all subsequent ones. The focus is on all humanity and the whole earth. Except for possibly a few minor exceptions, all the major and minor themes of the five stages find their origin here. In some cases, themes are only briefly mentioned or alluded to in embryonic form, only to be developed with greater detail and richness in later cycles. The careful reader of this cycle will be rewarded in reading the rest of Scripture.

1. Creation[1] (Gen 1–2)

Creation from chaos

As with every cycle, God creates order and life from chaos and death. Genesis 1:2 says that the earth was formless, void, dark, and covered in water, which elsewhere in Scripture is the language of death and chaos (e.g., Ps 88:12; Isa 34:11; Jer 4:23).[2] The verb 'create' used in Genesis 1:1 is a special one in the Hebrew Bible since only God is used as its subject, and thus this action refers

1. Cf. Stordalen, *Echoes of Eden*; Postell, *Adam as Israel*.

2. Isaiah 14:3–21 and Ezek 28:11–19 may be speaking of a pre-Adamic fall of the angels, which would in turn support the idea of creation from chaos. Satan's fall is due to pride, the mother of all sin (Ezek 28:17; 1 Tim 3:6).

to a unique creational activity in which God makes something new.[3] This is unique, divine creation, which will be the theme for all subsequent (re)creations throughout Scripture. Later texts will describe God's creation as him 'giving birth' to creation (e.g., Ps 90:2), which highlights his sovereign rule over creation, as well as his personal connection to it.

Creation battle

The mention of 'great sea creatures' in Genesis 1:21 evokes the idea of typical Ancient Near Eastern mythological creatures of chaos which must be subdued by the forces of order (Ps 148:7).[4] Although Genesis 1 is markedly different from other Ancient Near Eastern myths in that God is the sovereign creator of these monsters, later biblical texts will utilize the creation battle theme when speaking of God's creation in order to portray his ability to bring order out of chaos (e.g., Job 26:12–13; Ps 74:13–14; 89:10–11). It is *as if* God had battled with gigantic creatures of chaos when he created the cosmos.

God's Spirit

God's 'wind,' which is the same word for 'Spirit,' is mentioned in Genesis 1:2. God's wind/Spirit 'hovering' over the waters suggests not only his presence, but also his sovereignty. In subsequent cycles, God's wind/Spirit often will be associated with themes such as creation, deliverance, and salvation.[5]

3. However, other verbs are also used to describe God's creational activity (e.g., Ps 146:6).

4. The word 'deep' in Gen 1:2 is etymologically connected with Tiamat, the great sea monster of chaos known throughout the ANE. Elsewhere in Scripture, this creature is referred to as Leviathan, Tannin, Nahash, and Rahab (Job 7:12; 26:12–13; Ps 74:13–14; 89:10 [MT: 11]; Is 27:1; 51:9).

5. Here, the Spirit's relationship to water is negative since oceanic water represents chaos and death. Elsewhere his relationship is positive since rain and river water represent life (e.g., Isa 32:15; Ezek 36:25–26; Joel 2:28–29; John 3:5; 7:38–39).

God's word

God's spoken word is a prominent theme in Genesis 1, since he used the word to overcome formlessness and void (Ps 33:6). By his word, formlessness was formed and void was filled. In addition to noting *that* God spoke, it is also important to note *how many times* he spoke: ten.[6] God speaking ten times to give order and life will reappear in subsequent cycles. The number ten itself conveys the idea of completeness and reappears at several places throughout Scripture.

Temple

As an increasing number of scholars have noted, in Genesis 1 God is transforming the cosmos into a temple for man to dwell in (e.g., Ps 104:2; Job 9:8; Is 40:22).[7] The order in which God created is also suggestive: in Genesis 1:2, the cosmos was formless and void, and beginning in Genesis 1:3, God constructed this cosmic temple from the raw material of Genesis 1:2. This evokes the idea of victory plunder, in which rulers would build temples and other important buildings from the booty they won from their defeated enemies. Thus, it is *as if* God had built this temple with the victory plunder that he took from the forces of chaos (although it must be emphasized again that God has no peer, and there was no creation battle *per se*). Significantly, this is how subsequent temples will be built throughout the biblical story.[8]

6. The phrase "And God said" appears in Gen 1:3, 6, 9, 11, 14, 20, 24, 26, 28 (slightly different), 29. Genesis 1:22 has not been included since the verbal form is different (infinitive), nor has Gen 2:18, which contains a similar, yet distinct phrase ("And the LORD God said"), and anyways is found in a different context. For ancient support of this reading, cf. m. Avot 5:1; *ARN* 31 (neither of which cite texts); for modern support with texts, cf. Wenham, *Genesis 1–15*, 6; Matthews, *Genesis 1–11:26*, 117 n. 13; Gage, *Gospel of Genesis*, 39 n. 27.

7. For example, Walton, *Genesis 1 as Ancient Cosmology*. There are also various references in which the cosmos is described in house-like terms: e.g., Gen 7:11; Job 26:11; Ps 78:23.

8. Gage, *Gospel of Genesis* 22 n. 21. See subsequent cycles for references.

Also to be noticed is how God's temple was created from primordial chaos. In Genesis 1:2, chaos is described as 'formless' and 'void.' God overcame each component of this chaos in two sets of three days: during the first three days God overcame 'formlessness' by constructing the basic divisions of the cosmos, and during the following three days he overcame the 'void' by infusing each division with life.[9] This may reflect how the tabernacle and temple were structured: divided into three parts—outer court, holy place, most holy place—and then filled with corresponding temple furniture.

Rest

After creation was completed, God rested (Gen 2:1–3). Although the verb in Genesis 2:15 is typically translated as "placed," "put," or something similar ("God took the man and *put* him in the garden of Eden"), it comes from the verb 'rest' and is etymologically connected to the name 'Noah.' Thus, a literal translation of this verse could be: "God took the man and *caused him to rest* in the garden of Eden." This rest is not the same as physical inactivity, however, but rather refers to a deeper, spiritual rest which manifests itself in physical activity: God "caused [Adam] to rest" in the garden in order that he would 'work' and 'keep' it (Gen 2:15). Elsewhere in Scripture, these action verbs are typically used for priestly work carried out in the tabernacle and temple (e.g., Num 3:5–8). Hebrew readers most likely would have seen Adam's work in the garden as a kind of priestly service, and priestly work in the tabernacle and temple as a kind of creational service that was similar to what God had intended Adam to do.

9. The verbs of the first three days are predominately ones of separating and gathering raw material, whereas those of the next three days are predominately ones relating to the sprouting forth of new life.

2. Man (Gen 1–2)

Election

With chaos having been overcome, God made mankind (Gen 1:26–28), with Adam as representative (Gen 2:7, 15–18). Mankind was made in God's 'image,' and 'likeness,' which, along with whatever else these terms might mean, implies that they were to reproduce on earth what God had just finished doing throughout the cosmos. One of Adam's primary responsibilities was to care for the animals (Gen 2:18–19), and given the fact that his son Abel was a shepherd (Gen 4:2), it is plausible to suggest that, either before or after his expulsion from the garden, Adam was a shepherd, which will become the typical occupation for God's chosen men. Psalm 8:5 states that God made man "a little lower than the heavenly beings," which means that, from the very beginning, God established the pattern of choosing the younger and weaker over the older and stronger.[10]

Adam is the first of a handful of biblical characters to be portrayed as prophet (Gen 2:15–17; 3:2–3 [responsible for telling Eve what God had told him]), priest (Gen 2:15), and king (Gen 1:26–28; 2:18–23). Many subsequent biblical figures will be described as fulfilling the same roles.

Formed outside; 'go forth'

Adam was formed outside the garden and later placed in it (Gen 2:7–8).[11] This foreshadows similar events in subsequent cycles, in which God's elected man (or people) will be chosen outside of the Promised Land and then given the charge to 'go forth' and enter it.

10. This may even be seen to apply to topography: Mt. Hermon is visible from Jerusalem and almost three times higher. Yet, as Ps 68:15–16 says, it envies Jerusalem because it is God's chosen mountain.

11. During the first millennium or so of Christianity, authors posited three locations for Adam's creation: Jerusalem, Hebron, and Damascus, with Damascus and Hebron essentially fusing into one place (Hilhorst, "Ager Damascenus"). For our purposes, the exact location of Adam's creation is not as important as the simple fact that he was formed outside of the garden of Eden.

Mixed multitude

Since this is the first cycle, there is no clear evidence of a mixed multitude, unless the serpent is counted as such (see below). However, traditional Christian interpretation of Adam and Eve in the garden is that, while they were rational creatures and morally blameless, they had not yet achieved mature human reasoning and unbreakable moral uprightness. This lack of perfections made it possible for there to arise within them a mixed multitude of reasoning and volition. Nehemiah 13:3 illustrates why the concept of a mixed multitude is so detrimental: by contrasting the terms 'mixed' and 'separate,' the latter of which is a key creational term which brings order and makes life possible (Gen 1:4, 6–7, 14, 18), it implies that a mixing of good and evil, or of God's people with those who have rejected God, would be as disastrous as the light, sky, earth, and water returning to their original state of undivided chaos.

Mountain and garden

Adam was placed in the garden of Eden (Gen 2:8),[12] which was located on a mountain.[13] In the ancient worldview, earth was the

12. The word 'garden' used in Gen 2:8ff. is used in parallelism in Eccl 2:5 with another Hebrew word that can be translated as garden, orchard, or even forest, and is where the word "paradise" comes from. These words refer to a field—usually surrounded by a natural or man-made enclosure—with trees, bushes, and plants that were food-producing or otherwise beneficial for mankind (e.g., shade, timber), with a dependable water source nearby (river or well). Vineyards and olive, date, and fig trees were common features (Stordalen, *Echoes of Eden*, 36–38, 81–83). By way of contrast, in Isa 51:3 the words "garden" and "Eden" are contrasted with "waste places," "wilderness," and "desert."

13. That Eden was a mountain can be seen in four ways. First, water flowed out of Eden (Gen 2:10), which necessitates a raised topography. Second, Ezek 28:13–14 states that Eden was on a mountain. Third, nearly all ancient civilizations placed their garden-temples on mountains or high places, and its absence in the biblical record would be unexpected. Fourth, subsequent cycles will all include a mountain, thus implying that the first cycle had one as well. The religious aspect of high places—be they natural or manmade—is attested throughout the ancient world: the Greeks had Mount Olympus; the Romans

domain of mankind, sky was the domain of deity, and mountains were where the two came together. Mountains provided a unique situation in which the participant would be isolated from the world and thus able to direct the entirety of their being toward God, and at the same time able to comprehend their surroundings and see the whole of the task—physical and spiritual—that God had put before them. Mountains provide solid ground and physical distance from the waters of chaos below, and thus become emblematic of security and the establishment of order.

Also mentioned in the mountain-garden complex is the presence of rivers (Gen 2:10–14) and important trees (Gen 2:9, 16–17). Rivers will become emblematic of life since they provide drinkable water and make society possible for humanity (e.g., Ps 65:9).[14] Trees will become emblematic of life and blessing since they provide food and aspects of leisurely life, such as shade and aesthetic beauty (e.g., Ezek 31:3–9). The mountain-garden complex was to be the epicenter of civilization as humans expanded God's reign throughout the earth. It was to be the cradle of man's social, economic, technological, artistic, and religious endeavors. Thus, Eden would have been the first city founded by humans and the model for all subsequent ones. In Scripture, cities are seen as either mini-Edens or anti-Edens. Although there has been much debate about the location of Eden and its garden, numerous factors point to its conceptual and geographical overlap with the Promised Land in general, and Jerusalem in particular (see *Excursus* at the end of this chapter).

Divine blessing and commands

In Genesis 1:28, God 'blessed' mankind (cf. Gen 5:2) and charged them with five commands: 'be fruitful,' 'multiply,' 'fill,'

had Monte Cavo; the Syrians had Mount Casios; the Hindus had Mount Meru; the Egyptians, Mesopotamians, and Meso- and South Americans all built pyramids or ziggurats for religious purposes, in many cases because their terrain lacked natural mountains.

14. Nearly all ancient cities—and still most modern ones—were founded on the banks of rivers.

'subdue,' and 'have dominion.' This combination of blessing and commands is known as the Adamic covenant, which will become the basis for all subsequent covenants, many of which will make direct linguistic connections with Genesis 1:28. At a conceptual level, God has commanded mankind to reproduce on earth what he had completed doing with the cosmos: as God had overcome formlessness by ordering the cosmos during the first three days of creation and void by filling the cosmos during the next three days, so too was mankind charged to overcome the formlessness of the land outside of the garden of Eden by 'subduing' and 'having dominion' over it, and the void by 'being fruitful,' 'multiplying,' and 'filling' the earth.[15] Thus, all of Scripture's covenants are an invitation to replicate on earth God's creational activity. As subsequent cycles will show, when God's chosen person (or people) refuses to mirror God's creational activity on earth, it is an ominous sign that a fall is at hand.

3. Fall[16] (Gen 3)

Not vigilant

After God had established his covenant with mankind, they fell into sin (Gen 3:1–7). Although God had given them dominion over every creature, and every plant was theirs for food (Gen 1:28–29), Eve was deceived by the serpent (i.e., Satan[17]) and they both rebelled by eating the one tree that was forbidden (Gen 2:16–17; 3:1). Instead

15. These verbs appear to divide along gender lines: Adam is to establish order by primarily subduing and having dominion over the earth, and Eve is to give life primarily by being fruitful, multiplying, and filling the earth. Similar to how God rested, blessed, and sanctified the seventh day because of the fullness of order and life that he had brought through his creational activity, so too will human society be able to enjoy God's rest, blessing, and sanctification when they fulfill their respective tasks to bring order and life into the world.

16. Proverbs 7:6–27 seems to be a typological description of temptation, sin, and death. This text should be kept in mind throughout all the cycles.

17. For NT support, cf. Jn 8:44; Rom 16:20; 2 Cor 11:3; Rev 12:9; 20:2. The serpent is the prototypical enemy of God's people, especially Abraham's descendants. He is unexplainably in the land, just as the Canaanites were in the land as Abraham entered (Gen 12:6).

of 'working' and 'keeping' the garden—which included protecting it from any danger or threat—, Adam failed to remain vigilant, and thus the serpent was able to deceive his wife, who, in turn, handed the fruit to him, which he then ate (Gen 3:6).[18]

Woman; deception/seduction; usurpation

Eve was deceived by the serpent to choose death over life (Gen 3:1–6; cf. 2 Cor 11:3; 1 Tim 2:14). The story reads like a tragic deception, similar to how an evil adult might deceive an innocent child to commit a horrible deed. Although he never touched Adam and Eve physically, the serpent committed an act of murder (cf. Jn 8:44). Genesis 3:6 contains key words that describe Eve's mental and spiritual state, and which will recur frequently in connection with the fall of God's chosen person (or people): 'see,' 'good,' 'pleasant,' 'desire,' 'make wise,' and 'take.' As subsequent cycles will demonstrate, the wife of God's chosen man often will be seduced and/or forcibly taken by another man in an attempt to usurp the chosen man's rightful authority and to establish a rival kingdom.[19] This may have been the serpent's goal in seducing Eve away from God and her husband: to overthrow God's kingdom as it was mediated through Adam and to set up a rival kingdom in its place.

Hebrews 3:12–19 states that rebellion, sin, and disobedience are rooted in unbelief. Therefore, Adam and Eve's sin, as well as all subsequent sins, should be seen fundamentally as an act of unbelief in God which manifests itself in sinful works. The only way to deal with sin is by repentance and faith in God, which manifests itself in righteous works (cf. Gal 5:6).

18. This is more implied than stated in the case of Adam, but any ancient reader would find it highly irregular that a man would let his wife speak to a third party.

19. In ancient political theory, this is the mark of a tyrant: one who comes to power by unconstitutional means and appropriates for himself the power and riches of the previous constitutional ruler.

Knowledge of sin

As a result of their sin, Adam and Eve's eyes were opened and they 'knew' they were naked (Gen 3:7). This does not refer primarily to the physical sphere, otherwise their loincloths would have solved the problem (Gen 3:7). Rather this refers to the internal perception of the evil that they had committed and its shameful consequences.[20] This was the awful moment when they were confronted, all at once, with the full reality of their actions. They had been deceived into rebelling against God and bringing on themselves the curse of death. Their nakedness, which formerly had been a symbol of their purity, innocence, and intimacy (Gen 2:25), had become a symbol of their uncleanness, guilt, and alienation (Gen 3:7–10).

Curse

The fall into sin was followed by God's 'curse' (Gen 3:14–19). Just as the serpent had deceived Eve, who in turn gave the fruit to Adam, God 'curses' the serpent, Eve, and Adam in turn. Each curse corresponds to their natural state of blessing. Whereas the serpent had been the most 'clever' or 'cunning' of the animals, he would now be forced to slither on his belly, with his head placed near the dirt, and always in threat of being crushed by the (unclean) feet of another (Gen 3:14–15). Whereas the woman had been created as a 'helper' who was fit for Adam and as the mother of all life (Gen 2:18; 3:20), now the two will be locked in a constant struggle for power, and childbearing will be a painful experience (Gen 3:15). Whereas Adam had been created to rule over the earth and work and keep the land while in a state of rest, now the ground was 'cursed,' his labor became painful, and in the end the earth will prove to be his master (Gen 3:16–19).[21] The most terrifying consequence of all, however, was mankind's expulsion from God's presence (Gen 3:22–24). They were 'sent' and 'driven' from God's presence, and the way back to the garden was

20. Similarly, their physical hiding reflects their spiritual hiding.

21. In Gen 3:17, God 'curses' the ground, but it is clear from Gen 3:19 that this affects Adam as well.

guarded by a 'cherubs.' By introducing chaos into God's *moral* order, mankind had introduced chaos into God's *created* order, and the threat of cosmic formlessness and void will become a constant worry for mankind to contend with.

Forgiveness

Although God had righteously judged sin, he also showed deep mercy. First, he offered forgiveness, which from the beginning was not without the shedding of blood (Gen 3:21). Second, he offered the promise that one day the woman's seed would overcome that of the serpent (Gen 3:15). Just as the root of mankind's rebellion against God was unbelief, the root of mankind's return to God will be repentance and faith (cf. Gen 4:26). That Adam believed in God's promise is illustrated by his naming of Eve (Gen 3:20): he believed that she would be the mother of all living, which implied his faith that someday her seed would overcome the seed of the serpent.[22]

4. Division[23] (Gen 4–6)

Division

God foreknew that there would be perpetual conflict between the seeds of the woman and of the serpent (Gen 3:15), which is typified in the division between Cain and Abel (Gen 4:1–26; cf. 1 Jn 3:12) and later in the antediluvian generation (Gen 6:1–8).[24] Both seeds were guilty of sin and therefore deserving of death (Gen 5), but one repented and turned back to God while the other continued obstinately in rebellion. The division between the seeds, and the ever-narrowing focus of the one through whom God plans to

22. Waltke, *Genesis*, 95.

23. Seminal thoughts of some ideas stated here can be found in Irenaeus, *Demonstration*, 17.

24. This is not to imply that Cain and his descendants were the *physical* descendants of the serpent, but rather shared such traits to be considered his *spiritual* descendants.

bless the rest of creation, will become a major theme throughout Scripture, and will be a driving force behind the progression of the biblical story.

In addition to indicating the repentance or rebellion of the two seeds, Scripture will also mark their differences by assigning to them different occupations and animal imagery. As for occupations, sheepherding often marks God's people, especially his chosen ones (see below), and even God Himself is connected to this pastoral imagery.[25] The phrase "flowing with milk and honey," repeatedly used to describe the Promised Land, is a pastoral image that most likely refers to an abundance of goat's milk and bee's honey, which are signs of God's grace.[26] As for animal imagery, God's people will become associated with docile and defenseless creatures such as sheep (e.g., Ps 79:13), whereas God's enemies will become associated with filthy and violent animals, such as dogs, pigs, bulls, and lions (e.g., Ps 22:12–13; Matt 7:6).

Persecution

Cain's murder of Abel (Gen 4:8) will become emblematic of the older, stronger, unrighteous seed persecuting the younger, weaker, righteous one. Although the precise identity of the Nephilim is debated, what is clear is that they were powerful, wicked beings who, had they been left unchecked, would have completely filled the earth with violence (Gen 6:11–13). The older, wicked seed persecuting the younger, righteous one will become a repeated theme throughout Scripture, especially as Abraham and his godly descendants will be threatened, harassed, persecuted, and killed by their stronger, wicked enemies, such as Egypt, Philistia, Assyria, and Babylon.

25. Genesis 48:15; Ps 23:1; 28:9; 74:1; 79:13; 80:1; 95:7; Isa 40:11; Jer 31:10; Ezek 34.

26. Beitzel, *The Moody Atlas*, 49.

Cities[27]

Although God's original purpose for mankind to establish a city in the garden–temple complex had been (momentarily) frustrated, humans would continue to found cities, but instead of reflecting God's order and life they will reflect their founders' spiritual chaos and death. Eden had no walls, since all things would have been shared in common and there would have been no fear of attacks from foreign or domestic enemies, but anti-Edenic cities will build high, strong walls as their inhabitants seek to hoard riches for themselves and are perennially at war with each other.[28] The rebellious seed will be focused on building its own kingdom, 'naming' cities after themselves (Gen 4:17), whereas the repentant seed will be focused on God's kingdom, 'calling' on the Lord (Gen 4:26).[29]

Apostasy; inter-marriage

Although the precise meaning of the inter-marriage between the sons of God and daughters of men is still debated (Gen 6:1–4), what is clear is that the godly line was overcome by the ungodly one. If violence proves insufficient to do away with the godly line (Gen 6:5), then apostasy and inter-marriage—that is, spiritual and physical seduction—could be used, as the godly line would slowly lose its distinctiveness and cease to exist as God had intended (Gen 6:1–2). The twin sins of violence and lust—the chaotic counterparts to God's original command for mankind to have dominion and be fruitful—will become the primary means by which the godly line is neutralized, and the evil line will not stop until all their thoughts are evil and the whole world is filled

27. For a unique and insightful reflection on the idea the city, cf. Ellul, *The Meaning of the City*.

28. Gage helpfully comments, "[I]t is the pattern for the wicked to be the city builders, not the righteous. These cities of man portrayed in Genesis are but parodies of the true paradise" (*Gospel of Genesis*, 59).

29. The words translated 'name' (Gen 4:17) and 'call' (Gen 4:26) are the same in Hebrew, and the text offers a play on words.

with corruption and violence (Gen 6:5, 11–13).[30] The godly line slowly abandons its distinctiveness, with the result that the moral fabric which holds society together is slowly undone. When this happens, the flood waters of chaos begin to rise.

Prophet; preacher of righteousness

Some godly men like Enoch and Noah preached repentance, but it appears that few people listened to them (cf. 2 Pet 2:5; Jude 14–15). These prophets (in the technical and non-technical sense of the word) were God's way of showing patience to mankind, giving them ample warning to repent and return to him. Beginning with Enoch, the seventh generation will become an important indicator for identifying many of God's chosen men, including prophets and preachers of righteousness.[31]

Affliction; 'crying out'

In the Cain and Abel story, it is especially noteworthy that Abel's blood 'cried out' to God (Gen 4:10; cf. Heb 12:24). This will become the godly line's last resort against the relentless attacks of the ungodly. God's patience in sending prophets who denounce the wickedness of their day will come to an end when God determines to intervene. He will rescue his people and judge his enemies.

5. Judgment (Gen 6–7)

Chaos; flood

With the rebellious seed dominating the scene, God brought judgment in the form of a flood (Gen 6:1–7:24), which will become emblematic of chaos and judgment returning to earth (e.g., Ps

30. The sins of violence and sexual immorality are ubiquitous throughout the Bible and function as the two primary placeholders for other sins, the former including sin committed against others (i.e., malice), and the latter including sin committed against oneself (i.e., incontinence). Cain's paradigmatic sins of murder and polygamy in Gen 4 illustrate this.

31. Sasson, "A Genealogical 'Convention.'"

124:4–5). The flood is God's judgment on mankind that undoes his original creational order.[32]

Exile; expulsion

Mankind was cut off from earth, and all flesh died (Gen 7:21–23). As it will be expressed in the context of subsequent cycles, the earth's inhabitants had become so wicked that the earth could no longer bear them and vomited them out (cf. Lev 18:26–28). Earth would rather bear the physical waters of cosmic chaos than the spiritual waters of moral chaos that mankind had brought on it. It would rather drink the bitter waters of chaos than the shed blood of humans.

Deliverance of righteous remnant[33]

Only the small remnant of Noah and his household were saved, while the rest of mankind suffered judgment (Gen 6:17–18; 7:21–23). God's intervention will always bring this dual destiny for mankind: some will be saved, while others condemned. This is the astonishing reversal that Scripture bears witness to: the few, powerless, persecuted descendants of the woman will be fully vindicated one day, while the numerous, powerful, oppressive descendants of the serpent will be fully judged.

32. A key verb in this passage is 'destroy/corrupt,' which refers both to man's actions as well as the effects of the flood (Gen 6:11–13, 17; 9:11, 15). In Ps 16:10, the noun form of this word is found in parallel relationship to Sheol.

33. The idea of a remnant was also present in ANE literature and in many cases related to the survivors of the deluge; cf. Hasel, *The Remnant*, e.g., 51–58, 67–79. Hasel points to the importance of a remnant when he writes, "No remnant means no life, a remnant means life and existence. The remnant possesses the immense innate potentialities of renewal, regeneration, and restoration" (*The Remnant*, 384).

Excursus: On the Location of the Garden of Eden[1]

Regarding the location of the garden of Eden, there are several observations that suggest it was in the Promised Land, and most likely Jerusalem itself.[2] Here I list seven of them.

First, many passages describe Canaan in garden-like language, even comparing it to the garden of Eden.[3] In fact, some passages such as Isaiah 51:3 use Zion in poetic parallelism with Eden and the Garden of the Lord, thereby drawing a conceptual link between the two.

1. Ottosson, "Eden and the Land of Promise." According to etymology and comparative philology, Eden can mean "pleasure," "enrich," or "luxuriant" (Stordalen, *Echoes of Eden*, 257–61).

2. Apparently, this is a relatively novel suggestion. According to the literature cited by Stordalen, most commentators think that Eden was either a mythical or heavenly place, or that it was located somewhere in eastern Mesopotamia, such as Armenia or Babylon (*Echoes of Eden*, 251–56; but cf. 307–10). Stordalen himself hints at Sinai and Zion, but ultimately places it in "the other world" beyond what humans could reach today (*Echoes of Eden*, 285–86, 452–54). For authors who connect Eden with the Promised Land, cf. Sailhamer, *Pentateuch as Narrative*, 99; Postell, *Adam as Israel*, 88–92.

3. Genesis 13:10; Exod 3:8; Num 13:17–29; 14:7–8; Deut 1:25; 6:10–11; 8:7–10; 11:11–12; Josh 24:13; Ezek 20:6, 15; Neh 9:25.

Second, in the opening chapters of Genesis, each time that mankind sins, there is an eastward movement (3:24; 4:16; 11:2),[4] but when God calls Abram, it is the first westward movement in the book, and notably, he arrives at the Promised Land (Gen 12:1–5). This suggests that God's call of Abram was a kind of new creation (see below) which includes a geographic return to mankind's beginning in the garden.

Third, being that there are not many mountainous regions in the area where the Hebrew Scriptures were written, if Eden were a real place, then there would have been only a few possibilities where it could have been located. The mountainous region of Canaan suggests itself as one of the few possible options, and arguably as the best one, given Israel's history with the land there.

Fourth, there are numerous conceptual parallels between the garden and Canaan. For example, as God 'drove' Adam and Eve from the garden because of their sin (Gen 3:24), so also did he 'drive' the Canaanites from the Promised Land because of their sin (e.g., Deut 33:27; Josh 24:18). Similarly, as an angel was placed at the east of the garden to guard the way to the tree of life, so too did Jacob wrestle with an angelic figure, at which time his name was changed to Israel (Gen 3:24; 32:1, 24–32).[5]

Fifth, Genesis 1:14 speaks of the celestial bodies as being for signs and appointed times, which elsewhere in Scripture refers to Israel's festival calendar (e.g., Exod 13:10; 31:13). With the creation account being presented in a way to anticipate the presence of Israel in the Promised Land and Jerusalem, it would be difficult to imagine the Jewish people thinking that the feasts were celebrated in other cities such as Babylon or Egypt. Their celebration in the Promised Land, however, would make much more sense.

Sixth, Eden was the source of four rivers which apparently encompassed the known world. The number four is frequently

4. Notice, as well, the eastern cities mentioned in Gen 10–11: Babel, Nineveh, etc. As Stordalen concludes, "Clearly, in Genesis 1–11 movement towards the east is unfavourable" (*Echoes of Eden*, 268).

5. Several more parallels between the garden of Eden and the tabernacle and temple will be listed in subsequent chapters.

used in Scripture to convey the idea of universality and completeness, such as the four winds, four corners of the earth, and four living creatures under God's chariot-throne.[6] Thus, four world-encompassing rivers whose source originates in the same places suggests that the source is at the center of the world, which in this case would be Eden. The reason this is significant is because biblical and post-biblical tradition will see Jerusalem as the center of the world.[7]

Seventh, and building off the previous observation, the location of the four rivers that flow out of Eden suggests that the Promised Land was at its center since a plausible argument can be made that the four rivers surrounded the Promised Land.[8] The Pishon river flowed around Havilah, which Scripture associates with Arabia (Gen 25:18; 1 Sam 15:7), to the south and east of Canaan. The Gihon river flowed around Cush, which Scripture associates with Nubia or Ethiopia (2 Kgs 19:9), to the south and west of Canaan.[9] Finally, the Tigris and Euphrates rivers flowed to the north and east of Canaan.[10] This suggests that they shared a

6. Isaiah 11:12; Jer 49:36; Ezek 1:5ff; 37:9; Zech 6:5.

7. Ezekiel 5:5; 38:12 (cf. Judg 9:37: Mt. Gerazim); *1 Enoch* 26:1–2; *Jub.* 8:19 (although separating Eden from Jerusalem); Bodi, *The Book of Ezekiel*, 219–26. Apart from understanding the navel as the geographic center of the world, it could also convey the idea of a link between heaven and earth, which was how temples were viewed in the ancient world. In that case, Jacob's vision of the staircase at Bethel would be particularly illustrative (Gordon, *Holy Land, Holy City*, 31–33).

8. The four rivers are described with successively fewer words, thus implying that the readers were less familiar with the identities of the first two, Pishon and Gihon, and more familiar with the last two, Tigris and Euphrates. There is evidence that, at least in some cases, the names of rivers and oceans could be used interchangeably. This may help the identity of some rivers, such as Pishon, which may refer to the Red Sea and Arabian Ocean (Stordalen, *Echoes of Eden*, 278–79).

9. Some ancient Jewish texts identified the Nile as the Gihon river (e.g., Jer 2:18 LXX).

10. If the four corners view of the rivers is not persuasive, it may be that the four rivers delineated the extension of Israel's world as it related to the great empires of the time: the Tigris and Euphrates rivers referred to the extent of the Babylonian and Assyrian empires, and the Pishon and Gihon rivers to the

common, centrally-located source in Eden, which could be seen to coincide with some mountain in Canaan, with Jerusalem presenting itself as the most obvious candidate.

In summary, while the issue remains unsettled, there are several factors which suggest that the Promised Land, and particularly Jerusalem, is the best candidate for the location of the garden of Eden.

---

extent of the Egyptian empire. In this sense, the four rivers could still be seen to demarcate the known world.

Chapter 2: Noah, Representing Half of Mankind

Genesis 6–11

Ten generations after the creation of Adam, God re-created through Noah, who represented the godly line descended through Seth. Of the two lines of Adam, Noah is the only Sethite singled out as being righteous during the time immediately preceding the flood (Gen 6:8–9; 7:1). God has reduced his focus from all mankind throughout the whole world, to half of mankind living in a reduced geographical area, and as will be seen with Noah's descendants, this will be further reduced to a third of mankind living in even a smaller area.[1]

1. Creation (Gen 7–8)

Creation from chaos

As in the beginning when the earth was formless, void, lifeless, and covered in darkness, again the earth has been covered with the flood waters of chaos and filled with death, and the stormy skies have caused darkness to prevail (Gen 7:11–12, 18–23). The 'deep' once again covers the earth (Gen 7:11; 8:2). However, after

1. For this cycle as a whole (and its comparison to the previous one), cf. Sasson, "The 'Tower of Babel,'" 211–19; Rendsburg, *The Redaction of Genesis*, 7–25.

God 'remembered' Noah, slowly there began to appear signs of life and new creation: the waters subsided, mountains appeared, vegetation returned, and the earth began to sustain life once more (Gen 8:1, 3–5, 11–19). Male and female animals from the land and air were preserved on the ark (Gen 6:20; 7:14), which became a kind of floating mountain of order that was protected from the waters of chaos.

Although cosmic order had been reestablished, important defects remained: the original curses from Genesis 3:14–19 were carried over into the postdiluvian world, there was further alienation between man and animals (Gen 9:2–5a), and the violence that was characteristic of Cain and other antediluvians will continue to be a reality that must be dealt with (Gen 9:5b–6; cf. 8:21).

Creation battle

There is no mention in Genesis 7–8 of God's conflict with mythological creatures as part of his reestablishment of creational order (although he did overcome the Nephilim with the flood; cf. Gen 6:4), but later texts such as Psalm 29:10 will describe God as sitting victoriously on his throne over the flood,[2] thereby evoking the theme of battle and victory.

God's Spirit

As God's wind/Spirit hovered over the face of the waters in the beginning, God's 'wind' blows over the waters of the flood to turn back their chaotic destruction (Gen 8:1). Additionally, God will 'smell' the soothing aroma of the sacrifice (Gen 8:21), which is etymologically connected to 'wind/Spirit'.

2. This is the only text where the word "flood" is used outside of Gen 6–11.

God's word

As God had spoken ten times in Genesis 1 to order and fill the cosmos, he speaks ten times throughout the flood narrative of Genesis 6–9 to reestablish the cosmos.[3]

Temple

Upon leaving the ark, Noah built an 'altar' and offered up to God 'burnt offerings' of every 'clean' animal and bird, which God received as a 'soothing aroma.' All these words anticipate later vocabulary that will be used of the tabernacle and temple in relation to the sacrifices (e.g., Lev 2:12).[4] The picture we have is of an open-air temple, similar to the garden of Eden.

Rest

As God had rested on the seventh day of the first creation week (Gen 2:2), he now smells the 'soothing aroma' after the flood and is satiated (Gen 8:21). The phrase 'soothing aroma' could be translated literally as an 'aroma of rest' and is connected etymologically both to the word for Adam's 'rest' in Genesis 2:15 and to Noah's name.[5]

3. Genesis 6:3, 7, 13–21; 7:1–4; 8:15–17, 21–22; 9:1–7, 8–11, 12–16, 17. Admittedly there is greater diversity of expression than the uniformity of Gen 1—e.g., sometimes God speaks to Noah and sometimes to himself, both divine names ("God" and "LORD") are used, and two verbs for "said" are used—but the total figure of ten speech acts cannot be sheer coincidence within the context of Genesis, where the number ten is used so often throughout the book as a way to structure its contents at both micro- and macro-levels.

4. For several connections between the flood narrative and purification law in Lev (esp. ch. 14), cf. Sailhamer, *Pentateuch as Narrative*, 40–41.

5. The verb 'rest' is used in Gen 8:22 at the end of the creation stage, mimicking its earlier use in Gen 2:2–3 (but apparently with no further significance).

2. Man (Gen 6; 9)

Election

Noah was the only faithful remnant of the godly line (Gen 6:8–9; 7:1), and thus became the new man with whom God would renew his original covenant. He was called 'righteous' and 'blameless,' epithets which evoke Adam's pre-fall state (cf. Eccl 7:29) and that will be used later to describe other men with whom God will renew his covenant (e.g., Gen 17:1–2; 2 Sam 22:22–26).[6] Additionally, 'blameless' will be a term usually reserved for sacrifices, but which will also be used in connection with Abraham (Gen 17:1) and the pre-fall Lucifer (Ezek 28:15).[7] The point is that Noah has been chosen by God to fulfill the original creation mandate of Genesis 1:26–28. His intimate care for the animals makes him look like a shepherd (Gen 7:8–9, 15–16). His reception of revelation from God portrays him as a prophet (e.g., Gen 6:13–21), his sacrificial offerings convey his priestly role (Gen 8:20), and his position as father of the remnant community reflects his kingly status, as does the re-establishment of the creational blessing (Gen 9:1, 7) and his authority to bless and curse (Gen 9:24–27).

Formed outside; 'go forth'

Noah and his family 'go forth' from the ark in order to begin the recreation process (Gen 8:16–19). We do not know how far he traveled from the ark, but Scripture's silence on the matter suggests that he remained close to Mount Ararat. If so, this would be the only occasion where God's chosen man did not 'go forth' into the Promised Land.[8] Perhaps this is what Noah would have done had

6. These epithets are used in tandem on only two other occasions in the Hebrew Scriptures: in Ps 15:2 to describe the one who could ascend God's holy hill, and in Job 12:4, where Job described himself as a just and blameless man.

7. Butler, *Joshua 13–24*, 321.

8. It could be that Noah's apparent long-term residence at Mount Ararat went against God's command to 'fill' the earth (Gen 9:1), thereby foreshadowing in some ways the sin of Babel (Gen 11:1–9, esp. v. 4). Jewish tradition understood Melchizedek to be Shem; if true, this would place Noah's descendant

he not planted his vineyard and ceased being vigilant (see below). In this way, Mount Ararat may function similarly to Babel.

Mixed multitude

Despite the new creation, all is not as it should be. Noah himself was a fallen man, whose sinful tendencies will become evident as the narrative unfolds. Additionally, although in one sense God had established his covenant with Noah (Gen 6:18), in another sense he was working through Noah's entire family (Gen 9:1, 8), which would have included Ham. Externally, Ham was within the covenant community, but internally he was not. As subsequent cycles will show, this reflects the phenomenon of a mixed multitude, and to slightly adapt a phrase from Paul, not all who are descended from Noah belong to Noah (cf. Rom 9:6). Thus, there was a fatal flaw sown into the fabric of this cycle from the very beginning.

Mountain and garden

As Adam had been placed on a mountain in a garden, so too did Noah settle on a mountain, where he planted a vineyard (Gen 8:4; 9:20). Several early Jewish texts associate the tree of the knowledge of good and evil with a (grape) vine which, if true, would further link Adam's garden with Noah's vineyard.[9] Even if it is not true at a factual level, it may be seen as legitimate at a conceptual one: God has placed a new Adam on a new mountain in a new garden.

Divine blessing and commands

God reasserted his original blessing and commands (Gen 9:1–7),[10] and established his covenant with Noah, his descendants,

---

in the Promised Land.

9. *First En.* 32:4; b. Ber. 40a; San. 70a; *Mid. Rab. Gen.* 15:7; 19:5. For further discussion, cf. Brown, "The Mediterranean Vocabulary of the Vine," esp. 150, 170.

10. The Hebrew expressions in Gen 1:28 and 9:1 are very similar, and even identical in some places. The commands given to Noah have come to be known

and all living creatures (Gen 6:18; 9:9–17). This is known as the Noahic covenant.

3. Fall[11] (Gen 9)

Not vigilant

Instead of remaining vigilant and fulfilling God's commands to fill the earth, Noah became drunk with wine[12] and rendered himself powerless against the intrusion of evil (Gen 9:20–21).[13] Although the serpent's seed may have been wiped out in the flood, the terrifying truth was that, in some way or another, the serpent's seed dwelled in the hearts of the survivors of the flood. Thus, although Noah should have been even more vigilant to protect himself and his family from the evil that dwelled in their hearts, he failed to keep the newly established garden-temple safe from impurity and evil. Although God had clothed Adam and Eve (Gen 3:21), Noah 'uncovered' himself, and thus must be covered by others (Gen 9:21–23).

Woman; deception/seduction; usurpation

In a manner eerily reminiscent of the events recorded in Genesis 3:1–6, Noah's wife was overcome by another serpent-like figure: Ham.[14] The key interpretive expressions are found in Genesis 9:21–22, where it says that Noah was 'uncovered', and Ham 'saw' the 'nakedness' of his father. The expression "uncover the nakedness of [someone]" is found over two dozen times throughout the Old Testament, and on each occasion, it refers to having a sexual

as the Noahide laws. These first appear in *Jub.* 7:20 and are fully listed in t. Av. Zar. 8:4. They have resurfaced in Jewish and Christian literature ever since.

11. Sasson, 'The 'Tower of Babel,'" Tomasino, "History Repeats Itself."

12. In Lev 10:9, the Levites will be warned not to drink wine or fermented drink, both words being etymologically connected to Noah's account.

13. Both sins had to do with consuming fruit (Gen 3:2; 9:20).

14. For parallels between Noah's fall and Lot's sin (Gen 19:30–38), cf. Gage, *Gospel of Genesis*, 64 n. 3.

relationship either with that individual (less common) or his wife (much more common).[15] Careful readers of the text would not have missed the connection: Ham's sin was not seeing his father's naked body and reporting it to his brothers as so many modern interpreters maintain, but rather having a sexual relationship with either Noah or his wife and reporting it to his brothers. Based on the fact that Noah will curse Ham's *descendant* Canaan (Gen 9:25), the evidence strongly suggests that Noah's wife was the victim, with Ham either seducing or raping her. In light of the parallels with Genesis 3:1–6, Ham's intention was not primarily to fulfill any sexual fantasies—otherwise he probably would not have risked being found out by recounting his deed to his brothers (Gen 9:22)—, but rather to usurp Noah's authority, supplant him as ruler, and establish his own kingdom. His decision to recount his deed to his brothers most likely was his declaration that he had declared himself the new patriarch of the family.

Knowledge of sin

Noah's two other sons attempted to redress the situation through clothing (Gen 9:23), but as with Adam and Eve, the shame and nakedness was much deeper than purely physical. As Noah awoke from his drunken slumber (Gen 9:24), his internal eyes were opened, and he 'knew' the evil that had been done.

15. For the biblical usage, cf. Lev 18:6–19; 20:11, 17–18, 20–21; Deut 22:30; 27:20; Ezek 16:36–37; 22:10; 23:10, 18, 29. See also Ruth 3:9; Isa 47:3; Ezek 16:8; Neh 3:5. Exodus 20:26 has a different verbal construction, and most likely is discussing something other than sexual immorality. Leviticus 18:1–3 introduces the chapter in which are found many of the prohibitions to uncover a man's nakedness, and it connects such acts with the people of Egypt and Canaan, that is, two of Ham's descendants (Gen 10:6). Ancient commentators unanimously connected Ham's act with some sort of sexual immorality. For a defense of the interpretation presented here, cf. Bergsma and Hahn, "Noah's Nakedness."

Curse

Similar to the fate of the serpent and his seed, instead of establishing a dynastic line, Ham's descendant Canaan was 'cursed' to servanthood (Gen 9:25–27). As the seed of the serpent would be crushed by the seed of the woman, so too will the seed of Ham (Canaan) be crushed by the seed of Shem (Israel) during the conquest, which itself is an anticipation of the eschatological conflict between Satan's followers and God's people.[16]

Forgiveness

God did not judge Noah or his immediate family, but allowed them to live, become numerous, and spread over the earth (Gen 10). Noah showed that he had been forgiven by evoking a divine blessing over two of his children (Gen 9:26–27).

4. Division (Gen 9–11)

Division

As Adam and Eve's descendants had been divided into a godly, repentant seed and an evil, rebellious seed, Noah's descendants were divided into good and evil. Shem became the father of the godly line and Ham the father of the evil line, while Japheth played an ambiguous role, but one more closely associated with Shem than with Ham (Gen 9:24–27).[17] The three brothers and the peoples they represented were 'separated' over the face of the known world into their respective lands, languages, clans, and nations (Gen 10:5, 20, 31–32; cf. Deut 32:8).[18]

16. It is important to clarify that this cursing is not based primarily on physical genealogy, but rather on spiritual genealogy: those who oppress God's people are fulfilling the role of Ham and subsequently take on his curse. As the story progresses, it will become evident that all of humanity is spiritually a Hamite, a descendant of Cain, a citizen of Babylon, that must be redeemed in order to become a Shemite, a descendant of Abel, a citizen of Jerusalem.

17. Genesis 9:25 says that Ham will be a servant to his brothers, not just to Shem.

18. The unexpected order of Gen 10 coming before Gen 11 might be

Persecution

An examination of Ham's genealogy in Genesis 10:6–20 demonstrates that Israel's worst enemies and oppressors—Egyptians, Canaanites, Babylonians, Assyrians, and Philistines—were all his descendants.[19] This passage foreshadows Israel's future woes at the hands of her oppressors: as Cain had persecuted Abel, these nations will persecute Israel. During this current cycle, God's people were persecuted at the hands of the builders of cities, especially Babel.

Cities

Similar to how Cain had "settled in the land of Nod, east of Eden" and built the city Enoch (Gen 4:16–17), Shinar was located to the east of Jerusalem, where Babel was built (Gen 10:10; 11:2, 9). Babel was not simply an isolated tower in an open field, but rather the central point of a sprawling city complex. Babel and cities like it ought to be seen as anti-Edens, the incarnation of man's hubristic and rebellious spirit. The land of Shinar was a place associated with Ham's descendants (Gen 10:10) and the purpose of building the tower of Babel was to achieve immortality through long-lasting renown.[20] The building of great cities and towers was associated with warfare and slavery in the ancient world (cf. Gen 10:8–10), and thus it is likely that the manpower utilized to build the tower (Gen 11:3–4) was not from freemen who were hired for their

---

explained by the fact that, in order to follow the first cycle, the author was forced to arrange the events in this order, since division naturally comes before persecution and judgment.

19. Added to this list could be Esau's descendants such as the Edomites and Amalekites, since Esau took Canaanite (and Ishmaelite) wives (Gen 26:34; 28:6–9; 36:1–6).

20. This appears to be the purpose of all of mankind's fallen endeavors: to grasp at immortality in the face of mortality. This can only be achieved through works that will outlive one's lifetime, such as establishing a city and all that comes with it (e.g., wars, laws, culture). There may be a parallel between "men of renown" (Gen 6:4) and wanting to "make a name for ourselves" (Gen 11:4), especially since both demonstrate the great hubris of the wicked line.

labor, but rather from slaves who were forced to work in miserable conditions.[21] This situation foreshadows Egypt's treatment of the Israelites during their bondage (e.g., Exod 1:11–14).

Apostasy; inter-marriage

The expected presence of Shem's godly line in the narrative is conspicuously absent in the text, which may suggest that they had been oppressed, apostatized, or inter-married with non-Shemites. Joshua 24:2 states that Abraham and his ancestors worshipped other gods, and thus at some moment between Shem and Abraham, the godly line had become corrupt. Whatever the case may have been, Scripture's silence implies that there were few righteous people living in the world at this time.

Prophet; preacher of righteousness

Eber, the namesake of the Hebrew people, was the seventh descendant from Enoch, and the fourteenth descendant from Adam, thus making "Hebrew" the twice-seventh descendant from Adam, which surely is no coincidence.[22] Not much is said of him, but based on his genealogy, name, and position in the genealogical line, Scripture is gesturing toward his godly character. If there were anyone fulfilling the role similar to that of Enoch or Noah, it would have been Eber.

Affliction; 'crying out'

Although not explicitly mentioned in the text, we may assume that those who were being forced to build the tower of Babel were afflicted and crying out to God to be delivered from their suffering.

21. Marlowe, "The Sin of Shinar."

22. That is, according to the MT. According to the LXX, which includes Cainan between Arphaxad and Shelah, Eber would be the 15th generation from Adam and the 8th from Enoch.

5. Judgment (Gen 11)

Chaos; flood

Although mankind had been commanded to fill the earth both in the beginning and after the flood (Gen 1:28; 9:1), those at Babel were seeking the opposite (Gen 11:4), and thus their 'scattering' at the hand of God was an act of judgment against them (Gen 11:9).[23] Scattering and the confusion of language (Gen 11:7–9; cf. Deut 32:8) evoke the ideas of flood and chaos (cf. Gen 11:1), this time at a societal level. In fact, Scripture explicitly connects Babel with confusion (Gen 11:9). Having abandoned their uniting project of building the tower (Gen 11:8), mankind will now be separated and doomed to perpetual conflict with each other.

Exile; expulsion

As God had 'seen' the wickedness of mankind before the flood (Gen 6:5), again he comes down to 'see' their tower (Gen 11:5). With mankind being united in their rebellion, God judges them (Gen 11:5–9). They were "dispersed . . . over the face of all the earth" (Gen 11:9) and linguistically exiled from one another.

Deliverance of righteous remnant

Whereas Israel's worst enemies will come from the descendants of Ham, the Israelites themselves will come from Shem (Gen 10:21, 24). It is from this line that God will preserve a faithful remnant from whom he will recreate a new people. God established national boundaries for the various peoples which, although 'separating' mankind from each other, also functioned to protect the weaker nations and inhibit the stronger ones that would seek to expand their empires (Deut 32:8; Acts 17:26).

23. The only previous usage of the verb 'scatter' is in Gen 10:18 with reference to the Canaanites, thereby strengthening the verb's connotation of judgment.

Chapter 3: Abraham, Representing One Nation of Mankind

Genesis 12–36

TEN GENERATIONS AFTER NOAH, God recreated through Abraham[1] and his descendants, Isaac and Jacob. Of the seventy nations mentioned in Genesis 10, only Eber's descendant Abraham was chosen by God to be the one through whom he would bless the rest of creation. The name Eber is etymologically related to the gentilic Hebrew, which occurs for the first time in the Bible when referring to Abraham (Gen 14:13). Of the seventy nations mentioned in Genesis 10, Israel and her closest neighbors—Ammon, Moab, the Arabian peoples, and the Edomites—are curiously absent. This is an intentional omission on the part of the author at this point in the narrative, as he plans to devote the rest of the book of Genesis to narrowing and specifying God's chosen line—Abraham, Isaac, and Jacob—and distinguishing it from other familial, but ultimately rejected, lines—the descendants of Lot, Ishmael, and Esau.[2] Near the end of the book, two of Jacob's descendants—Joseph (Ephraim) and Judah—will rise to prominence, and will prepare the way for further reduction in subsequent cycles.

1. For the sake of consistency, I will use the name "Abraham" throughout (cf. Gen 17:5).

2. Dicou, *Edom*, 126–29.

Cullmann's idea of the election of a minority for the redemption of the whole becomes increasingly evident from this point on. The geographic focus also reduces to a portion of land between the Euphrates and Nile rivers (Gen 15:18–21).

1. Creation (Gen 12)

Creation from chaos

With the closure of the story of Babel, humanity has been dispersed throughout the world as a judgment for their hubristic act of defiance against God (Gen 11:9). They are no longer unified, but rather each nation seeks its own advancement at the expense of others. Specifically with respect to the circumstances of Abraham, several features evoke the idea of creation out of death, darkness, and void: Abraham and his family have been serving other gods, and thus are spiritually dead (Gen 11:28; Josh 24:2); Abraham's wife is barren and lacks the power to give life, and thus they are, as Hebrews 11:12 says, physically "as good as dead" (Gen 11:30; cf. 25:21; 29:31); the family's legal status is that of sojourners, and thus are legally dead (Gen 12:1–9); the land is suffering under a famine, and thus is agriculturally dead and void (Gen 12:10); and the Canaanites are present in the land, and thus the land is spiritually dead, dark, and void (Gen 12:6).

Creation battle

There is no obvious creation battle with the calling of Abraham. Rather, God will simply speak and create (see below).

God's Spirit

God's many appearances to Abraham imply his personal, sovereign presence, which overlaps with the role of God's Spirit.[3]

3. Genesis 12:7; 15:1, 17; 17:1, 22; 18:1, 22, 33. Also, God sent his angel to go before Abraham's servant while on his important task to find a wife for Isaac (Gen 24:7, 40).

God's word

As God had spoken at creation, God speaks again and calls forth a new creation: Abraham and his descendants. As God had spoken ten times at creation, on ten separate occasions he promises land and offspring to Abraham, Isaac, and Jacob.[4]

Temple

At least five features in Genesis 12:6–7 suggest that Abraham travelled to a holy place (Shechem) in Canaan, thereby placing him in a kind of outdoor temple. The expression "the place" (Gen 12:6) probably suggests a holy place.[5] Oaks were common sites for religious practices. Shechem will become an important civil and religious site amongst the Israelites (e.g., Josh 24:1; Judg 9:6; 1 Kgs 12:1). "Moreh" (Gen 12:6) literally means "teacher" and thus could be associated with an oracle of some kind. Finally, Abraham built an altar and God appeared to him.

4. The ten references are: Gen 12:1–7; 13:14–17; 15:1–21; 17:1–21; 18:17–19; 22:15–18; 26:2–5; 26:24; 28:13–15; 35:11–12 (Gen 22:7; 46:3; 48:4 are not counted because they are either third-person recountings of the promise or have a different focus). Texts such as Exod 6:3–4 unite these three patriarchs, thereby justifying treating them together here. Three other scenarios of the ten speech acts are possible. First, it could be argued that God spoke to Abraham on ten different occasions (Gen 12:1–3, 6–7; 13:14–17; 15:1–5, 7–21; 17:1–21; 18:9–15, 16–33; 21:8–14; 22:1–19). While this is possible, it does not seem as significant as the other scenarios. Second, it could be argued that God promised to give land and offspring to Abraham on ten separate occasions (Gen 12:1–3; 12:6–7; 13:14–17; 15:1–5; 15:7–21; 17:1–21; 18:17–19; 21:12 [?]; 22:15–18; 24:7 [?]). However, the references in Gen 21:12; 24:7 are a bit weak. Third, it could be argued similarly that God promised to give land and offspring to Abraham on ten separate occasions, some of which include promises made to Hagar and her descendants (Gen 12:1–3; 12:6–7; 13:14–17; 15:1–5; 15:7–21; 16:10; 17:1–21; 18:17–19; 21:12–13, 18; 22:15–18). Here the weaker references in the previous example have been removed, but it seems odd to include promises made to Hagar, Ishmael, and Ishmael's descendants. For an exhaustive list of all references and allusions to the Abrahamic promises (full or partial), cf. Clines, *The Theme of the Pentateuch*, 31–43.

5. Wenham, *Genesis 1–15*, 279.

Rest

There are no explicit references to God's rest, but there are some indications of it. As God rested after he had formed Adam outside of the garden and placed him in it, so too may God be resting after having called Abraham from Babylon and placed him in the new garden, the Promised Land. Also, Genesis 12:7–8 speaks of an intimate relationship between Abraham and God, which at least hints at the idea that God is at rest in this new circumstance.

2. Man (esp. Gen 12)

Election

Abraham was the only descendent of Eber that God chose, and he promised to make Abraham into a great nation (Gen 12:1–3). Abraham is portrayed as a man of faith and obedience (Gen 12:4) and is said to be God's servant and friend (Ps 105:6, 42; Is 41:8; 2 Chr 20:7). Abraham was a shepherd (Gen 12:16; 20:14; 21:27),[6] as were the twelve patriarchs after him (e.g., Gen 47:3).[7] Abraham was the seventh descendant from Eber, and either the 20th or 21st descendant from Adam, both of which would be important numbers (3 x 7 or 2 x 10).[8] As with Adam and Noah before him, Abraham was a prophet (Gen 15:1; 20:7), priest (e.g., Gen 12:7; 13:4), and king (Gen 14:13–16; 23:6).

6. Abraham's great-great-grandfather was named Reu which is etymologically similar to the word shepherd (Gen 11:18–21).

7. Laban and his family were also shepherds (Gen 29:9–10), thereby implying that Abraham's trade was a familial one. As 1 Chr 4:39–41 illustrates, at least some Israelites will continue to shepherd at least until the days of King Hezekiah.

8. According to the MT, Abraham was the 20th descendent from Adam, but according to the LXX, he was the 21st (the LXX includes Cainan between Arphaxad and Shelah). Additionally, if the ten *toledoth* of Genesis are arranged in parallel structure (1, 2, 3, 4, 5, 1', 2', 3', 4', 5'), Abraham, as the main character of the sixth *toledoth*, would be situated as a kind of second Adam within the book of Genesis, thereby increasing the connections between the two.

Formed outside; 'go forth'

Abraham was called from Ur of the Chaldees—a land associated with the chaos of Babel (Gen 10:10; 11:2)—and he and his family 'went forth' to Canaan (Gen 11:31; 12:4–5). It is significant to note Abraham's westward travel (Gen 12:4–5): until now, mankind's movement had been eastward and was associated with their sin (Gen 3:24; 4:16; 11:2),[9] but now God has called Abraham westward to the land of Canaan. At a narrative level, therefore, Abraham's westward movement is a return to Eden (see the *Excursus* in chapter 1).

Mixed multitude

Coming out of Babylon with Abraham were others who did not share Abraham's allegiance to the Lord. Abraham's father, Terah, settled in Haran instead of continuing to Canaan (Gen 11:31). Abraham's nephew, Lot, settled near Sodom and Gomorrah and ended up fathering children with his two daughters (Gen 19:30–38). Abraham's household members, Hagar and Ishmael, would not form part of God's promised line (Gen 17:18–21).

Mountain and garden

Abraham's initial sojourning was in the central mountainous region of Canaan, specifically Moreh and Bethel (Gen 12:6, 8).[10] Later in life, Abraham will bind Isaac at Mount Moriah, which later will be identified as the temple mount in Jerusalem (Gen

9. This pattern continues even after Abraham's westward journey (Gen 13:11; 25:6).

10. Although the text itself does not say that Moreh is on a mountain, other texts associate it with mountainous sites such as Shechem, Mount Gerizim, and Mount Ebal (Gen 12:6; Deut 11:29–30). Bethel—also located on a mountain (Gen 12:8; Josh 16:1)—is the primary place of God's dwelling during the Patriarchal period (Gen 12:8; 13:3–4; 28:19; 31:13; 35:1, 3, 15; Hos 12:4). Later, however, it will change into an idolatrous worship site for the northern kingdom (1 Kgs 12:26–29; 2 Kgs 17:28; Jer 48:13).

22:2, 14; 2 Chr 3:1).[11] As was noted in the *Excursus* in chapter 1, Canaan is frequently described with garden-like terminology, and Abraham's presence at the oak of Moreh also gestures toward a garden-like setting (Gen 12:6; 13:18; 18:1).[12]

Divine blessing and commands

God promised to make Abraham a mighty 'nation' through whom all other nations would be blessed (Gen 12:1–3). Similar to Genesis 1:26–28 where mankind was made in God's image and commanded to be fruitful and subdue the earth, God promised to grant Abraham a relationship with himself and to grant him posterity and land (cf. Gen 17:1–8; Isa 51:2).[13] It is important to note that the Abrahamic blessing and commands were repeated to Isaac (Gen 26:2–5; cf. 25:11), Jacob (Gen 27:27–29; 28:1–4, 13–15; 35:11–12; 46:2–4), and Joseph's descendants (Gen 48:15–20), which suggests that, while this new cycle began with Abraham, it continues throughout the entire patriarchal narrative.[14] This blessing–command–promise cluster is known as the Abrahamic covenant.

11. Abraham also had an encounter with Melchizedek, king of Salem, which may be associated with Jerusalem (Gen 14:17–20).

12. The tree feature resurfaces in the life of Abraham again in Gen 21:33, also in a religious context.

13. David Clines groups the patriarchal blessings into three: posterity, relationship with God, and land (*Theme of the Pentateuch*, 27). Related to God's initial covenant with Abraham (Gen 12:1–3), God established two additional covenants with him, one focusing more on land (Gen 15:7–21) and the other more on descendants (Gen 17:1–14). It should not go unnoticed that in Gen 15:17—within the context of God bringing Abraham's descendants out of Egypt—God's presence is represented by a pillar of smoke and a flaming torch, which will be the same representations of God during and after the Exodus (Exod 13:21–22).

14. Other factors point to their unity. First, the repeated refrain "The God of Abraham, Isaac, and Jacob" treats them as a collective whole (cf. esp. Ps 105:8–11). Second, they all experienced similar circumstances, such as having barren wives (Gen 11:30; 25:21; 29:31), experiencing famine in Canaan and travelling, or being tempted to travel, to Egypt (Gen 12:10; 26:1–2; 42:5; 46:6–7), and building altars to the Lord (Gen 12:7–8; 26:25; 33:20). It should

3. Fall (Gen 27)

Whereas in the previous two cycles, the man with whom God had made the covenant was the same man who fell, in this cycle the stages of man, fall, and division are divided amongst the three patriarchs: Abraham is the one with whom God established his covenant, Isaac is the one who will have the decisive fall, and Jacob and Esau will represent the division of the seeds.[15] While at first this may be a difficult proposition to accept, the linguistic and thematic parallels between Adam's and Abraham's creation, Eve's and Isaac's fall, and Jacob and Esau's clear role as the representative of Israel and the Gentiles, respectively, makes this a likely reading of the story. Treating the patriarchal story as a whole also parallels what was noted above in the theme "God's word": the fact that God repeated his divine blessing and commands ten times to Abraham, Isaac, and Jacob suggests that, at least in some way, these three patriarchs function as a whole.

---

not go unnoticed that the two stages of creation and fall overlap and are developed simultaneously: it is as if to suggest that the patriarchs were imperfect keepers of God's covenant from the very beginning, a theme that will be seen in other cycles.

15. The patriarchal fall is admittedly the hardest theme to identify in this cycle, but the most satisfying solution is the one presented here. Abraham's fall in begetting Ishmael through Hagar presents itself as a likely contender, and this duality was even interpreted as having major theological significance by Paul (Gal 4:21–31; cf. Sailhamer, *Pentateuch as Narrative*, 153–54), but for reasons to be explained below, it does not appear to be the major turning point in the patriarchal narrative. In short, Esau assimilates Ishmael into his symbolic role as the representative of the nations; Ishmael's story, therefore, is a foreshadowing of Esau's. Having said that, the numerous parallels between Ishmael and Esau should be noticed: both were born first, but neither could be the firstborn; both were loved by their fathers who wanted them to be the heir (Gen 17:18; 25:28), and yet this was opposed by God (Gen 17:19; 25:23) and their wives (Gen 21:10–12; 25:28); both ended up living in relatively less fertile areas (Gen 16:12; 27:39–40); both became fathers of prospering nations (Gen 21:13, 18; 36); and Esau married one of Ishmael's daughters (Gen 28:6–9). For these and other comparisons, cf. Dicou, *Edom*, 133–34.

Not vigilant

The book of Genesis is divided into ten sections, each beginning with the phrase "These are the generations of," followed by the story of the named individual's most prominent descendent. Thus, for example, in Genesis 11:27, the section begins "Now these are the generations of Terah," and recounts the story of Abraham. It is remarkable, therefore, that there is no section in Genesis that begins with the phrase "These are the generations of Abraham," which would naturally have recounted the story of Isaac.[16] In such a carefully crafted book as Genesis, such a gloss cannot be incidental, and Isaac must have been deemed as unworthy to receive such a focused treatment. The most likely explanation of this fact is that whereas in Isaac's early years he had been vigilant, after his twin sons Esau and Jacob were born, he ceased being vigilant and began to stray.[17] Thus, although God had given a clear prophecy regarding the destiny of Isaac's twin sons (Gen 25:23), and although Esau had taken for himself Canaanite wives,[18] Isaac continued to favor Esau (Gen 25:28; 27:1–4).[19] The reference to Isaac's visual impairment in Genesis 27:1 is more than a remark on his physical condition: he no longer can see spiritual truth clearly. The word translated "delicious food" is used six times in Genesis 27.[20] Isaac's obsession with "delicious food" echoes Esau's myopic vision of preferring Jacob's stew over his own birthright

16. Isaac is only a main character in Gen 26; elsewhere, he plays a secondary role.

17. Waltke, *Genesis*, 351; *Old Testament Theology*, 122, 338–42. The change happened when Isaac was sixty years old (Gen 25:26). Also, while Scripture frequently refers to God's people by the metonymies of Abraham and Jacob, it never does so by that of Isaac.

18. Genesis 26:34–35; cf. 27:46; 28:8–9; 36:1–6.

19. The text implies that Isaac planned to bless Esau privately (Gen 27:6; cf. 49:1–2), thereby suggesting a certain amount of self-doubt and shame on Isaac's part. Isaac (and his wife Rebekah) drops out of the Genesis narrative until the mention of his death in Gen 35:27–29, a deafening silence like that of his omitted *toledoth*.

20. It is only used twice more in the OT. For more examples, cf. Waltke, *Old Testament Theology*, 341.

(Gen 25:29–34). Just as previous sin had been connected with tempting food, so too was Isaac's.

Woman; deception/seduction; usurpation

Isaac has been seduced by Esau and his own base appetites to prefer delicious food over obeying God. On three separate occasions in Genesis 27 the text says that Isaac "loves" this delicious food (vv. 9, 14, 18), which is the same word used to describe his earlier love for his wife Rebekah (Gen 24:67). Esau was on the verge of usurping the blessing and birthright that rightfully belonged to Jacob, but Jacob deceived both Esau and Isaac, and obtained what was rightfully his (Gen 25:29–34; 27:1–29).[21]

Knowledge of sin

Isaac's violent trembling upon his realization that he had blessed Jacob instead of Esau indicates that his internal eyes were being opened to the truth of what had happened, and that he was fearful as Adam and Eve had been before him (Gen 27:33; cf. Gen 3:8–10). He attempted to redress the situation by offering another blessing for Esau (Gen 27:39–40), but it was to no more avail than Adam and Eve's attempt to cover themselves with fig leaves. There is, of course, a great irony to this: Isaac trembled because he had fulfilled God's will despite his determination not to do so.

Curse

Similar to the garden episode, Isaac's deception was followed by Esau being cursed.[22]

21. There is a sense of irony here in that Jacob must deceive his father and brother, which is typically the role of the serpent figure. This is not lost on the biblical authors, as Jer 9:4 demonstrates. Separately, perhaps it is significant that Jacob fears a curse will fall on him for what he will do (Gen 27:12–13).

22. Genesis 27:37–40. There may be an ironic play with the clothing feature in this account: the clothing that Isaac touched and smelled on Jacob would later be his source of shame.

Forgiveness

The fact that Isaac eventually recognized Jacob as the heir of the Abrahamic covenantal blessing implies that he had repented of his sin and been forgiven by God (Gen 28:1–4).

4. Division[23] (Gen 27–32)

The division between the seeds is not as obvious here as it is in other cycles, but two important observations suggest that the major division occurred between Esau and Jacob. First, Genesis 25:22–23 says that two nations were struggling in Rebekah's womb, and that they would be divided from each other. This prophecy foreshadows the rest of their relationship, which is unique in the patriarchal narratives. Second, the division between Jacob and Esau completes the long story of division that began in Genesis 11. In Genesis 10, all the nations of the known world were mentioned except for those that could trace their lineage back to Abraham and his family: the Israelites, Ammonites, Moabites, Arabian tribes, and Edomites. Therefore, what Genesis 10 had done at a universal level by dividing mankind into three groups and seventy nations, of which Eber has been seen to be the chosen line, Genesis 11–36 now does at a regional level by further specifying which "Eber-ites" God will choose to bless the world. Although Genesis 12:1–3 had made it clear that the Adamic and Noahic blessings were being passed on to Abraham, it was not clear to which of Abraham's heirs it was being passed. Thus, regarding the inheritance of the blessing, Lot, Ishmael, and Esau become the foils for Abraham, Isaac, and Jacob. In this way, Genesis 11–36 is a continuation of Genesis 10 and brings it to its logical conclusion: as God had chosen Shem and Eber's line amongst the many nations, he now chooses Abraham, Isaac, and Jacob amongst the Ammonites, Moabites, Arabians, and Edomites. The name "Israel" appears for the first time in Scripture in Genesis 32:28, when Jacob was given his new name, and thus Esau—the last foil in working out the Israelite line—is seen as Israel's closest nemesis. He functions as the representative of the

23. Dicou, *Edom*.

nations, the fountain from which God's non-chosen lines begin.[24] Therefore, the division between Jacob and Esau is the last division that the author of Genesis makes in his narrative, which comes to represent the beginning of the differentiation between Israel and the Gentiles (see below).

Division

As in previous cycles, Abraham's descendants are divided into a rebellious, wicked line and a repentant, godly line. Continuing the line of argumentation from above, although some division has already been seen between Abraham and Isaac on the one hand and Lot and Ishmael on the other, it is seen most clearly between Esau and Jacob (Gen 25:23–28; 27:1–46; cf. Josh 24:4).[25] Esau and Jacob were set over against each other and in many ways were exact opposites: they struggled with each other in the womb (Gen 25:23–26), had different physical characteristics (Gen 25:25–26; 27:11), had different occupations (Gen 25:27), were loved by different parents (Gen 25:28), received different blessings (Gen 27:26–29, 38–40), married different kinds of women (Gen 26:34–35; 28:1–2, 6–9), and had very different relationships with God (Mal 1:2–3). The reason for this is because Esau and Jacob represent the Edomites and Israelites, respectively (Gen 25:23, 30; 32:28), and the Edomites, in turn, represent the Gentile nations that will be hostile to Israel.[26] In short, Jacob and Esau depict Israel and the Gentiles, respectively. Just as God had

24. Dicou, *Edom*, 126–29, 150–53. As Dicou summarizes, "Edom, Israel's brother, became Israel's counterpart, 'the last of the nations'" (*Edom*, 200).

25. Note, however, that the division theme also appears between Ishmael and Isaac (cf. Gal 4:29) and between Joseph and his brothers (Gen 37:12–36).

26. Bert Dicou writes: "in Genesis Edom, just as in the prophetic books, represents the nations, and serves as Israel's opponent" (*Edom*, 16). Similarly, Bruce Cresson writes, "Moab, Ammon, Tyre, Philistia, Egypt, and others are condemned in the Old Testament with some regularity; but none of these approaches the position of Edom in this respect. The literary attestation of the Old Testament is that Edom was the most hated of all Israel's neighbors and, indeed, became a symbol for the enemies of God's people" ("The condemnation of Edom," 144–45).

'separated' the nations in Genesis 10 (cf. Deut 32:8), here again he 'separated' Jacob from Esau (Gen 25:23).

Similar to previous cycles in which the husband and wife gave birth to two sons who would represent the seeds of the woman and serpent, Isaac and Rebekah gave birth to Esau and Isaac. Thus, the serpent's seed, typified in Esau, was poised to bruise the heel of the woman's seed, typified in Jacob (a play on words in Hebrew[27]), but it was the latter who ultimately will crush the head of the former.

Persecution

After Isaac blessed Jacob, Esau vowed to kill his brother, which forced Jacob to abandon Canaan for Paddan-Aram (Gen 27:41–45; 28:5). Esau married Canaanite and Ishmaelite women and became the father of some of Israel's worst enemies, most notably the Edomites (Gen 36:9, 19, 43).[28] The very name "Edom"—meaning "red"—reflects Esau's base appetites (Gen 25:30) and his hairiness makes him look animal-like.[29] In contrast to Esau, Jacob became Israel's namesake and is the Lord's possession (Gen 32:28; 35:9–10; Deut 32:9). Jacob's new name is connected with the idea of striving with God and with men, which suggests an identity of hardship and even persecution, which can only be countered with prayer.[30] Although Esau never fulfilled his desire to kill Jacob (gen 27:41), Jacob lived in fear of the possibility: on the eve of their climactic reunion, Jacob was preparing for a personal scale of destruction

27. Genesis 3:15; 25:26; 27:36. In Hebrew, the word "heel" and the name "Jacob" are etymologically connected. Also provocative is the use of the word "heel" in Ps 41:9, which is quoted in the NT with reference to the betrayal of Jesus (Jn 13:18).

28. Esau was also the progenitor of the Amalekites, on whom God swore perpetual war (Gen 36:12; Exod 17:8–16).

29. Waltke, *Old Testament Theology*, 341.

30. More persecution could be mentioned. Laban treated Jacob unfairly, cheating him out of his rightful spouse and hired wages (Gen 29:21–30; 31:6–7, 41). Upon returning to Canaan, in a story reminiscent of the antediluvian sons of God, Shechem 'saw' Jacob's daughter Dinah, 'took' her, and raped her (Gen 34:1–2).

that would be reminiscent of a flood, and was trying to ensure that at least a remnant would survive (Gen 32:7–8, 11).

Cities

Similar to Cain, Esau built a city and called it Edom. While the former named the city after his son, Esau named it after himself (Gen 25:30; 36:8). In stark contrast, Jacob named places after his encounters with God and angels: Bethel (Gen 28:18–19; 35:14–15), Mahanaim (Gen 32:2), and Peniel/Penuel (Gen 32:30–31).[31] Thus, he is not seeking to make a name for himself, but rather to increase God's glory. Jacob did not build a city by oppressing his neighbors, but rather worked diligently and intelligently, and increased his wealth (Gen 30:25–43). His large quantities of servants and domesticated animals evoke the ideal garden-city, with Jacob as its head (Gen 30:43; 32:5, 13–15).

Apostasy; inter-marriage

Notably, there is not much evidence of apostasy and inter-marriage in this cycle. Continuing in the line of Abraham, Isaac and Rebekah forbade Jacob to marry a Canaanite woman and insisted that he marry from Abraham's family (Gen 24:1–3, 37; 27:46–28:1).[32] Esau offered to mix his company with Jacob's, but Jacob declined (Gen 33:12–17). Hamor the Hivite offered Jacob full inter-marriage between the two peoples, with the hope that the two would become one and that all Jacob's possessions would be theirs, but Simeon and Levi slaughtered the whole clan, which prohibited the union from happening (Gen 34). Laban tried to keep Jacob in

31. He also purchased land in Shechem, built an altar, and named it El-Elohe-Israel (Gen 33:20).

32. In contrast, Ishmael and Esau showed their further distancing from God's chosen line by not returning to Abraham's birthplace to take a wife, but rather marrying Egyptian and Canaanite women (Gen 21:21; 26:34–35; 28:8–9; 36:2). It is uncertain where Lot's wife came from, but the fact that she remains unnamed in the biblical text and mourned Sodom and Gomorrah's destruction suggests that she was not from Abraham's birthplace (Gen 19:26).

Paddan-Aram, which would have implied Jacob's disbelief in the LORD's promises to bring him back to Canaan (Gen 28:13–15), but he ultimately refused the offer and returned home.

Potential evidence of apostasy would be Rachel's theft of her father's household gods—which she simultaneously defiled by sitting on them while she was menstrually impure (Gen 31:19, 34–35)—and some foreign gods that Jacob and his sons had in their possession (Gen 35:2, 4). A more convincing example of apostasy is the only given case of inter-marriage: Judah's marriage to a Canaanite (Gen 38:1–5; 2 Chr 2:3). What is notable, however, is that the promised seed does not pass through the Canaanite woman, but rather through the fruit of Judah's affair with Tamar (Perez).[33]

Prophet; preacher of righteousness

There do not appear to be any prophets or preachers of righteousness during this period. Perhaps this is because God himself was more active in the narrative, and thus he speaks directly to the patriarchs.

Affliction; 'crying out'

Jacob was afflicted by Laban (Gen 31:42). Esau met Jacob with 400 men (Gen 32:6), and Jacob's last words from his brother had been that he wanted to kill him (Gen 27:41). In response, Jacob cried out to God for help (Gen 32:9–12).

33. The fact that Tamar is not said to be a Canaanite suggests that she was not one, in contrast to Judah's wife who is identified as Canaanite. Perez was the younger twin of Zerah but nevertheless was counted as the firstborn (Num 26:20–21). This is yet another example of the younger being preferred to the older.

5. Judgment (Gen 33–36)

Chaos; flood

While there is no immediate judgment for Esau and the Edomites, later biblical testimony is much more pessimistic.[34] In Numbers 24:15–19, Balaam says that one day Edom (and Moab) will be dispossessed, apparently at the hands of Israel. In Jeremiah 48–49, Lot's descendants are given promises of restoration (cf. Jer 48:47; 49:6), but the Edomites are not (Jer 49:7–22). In Lamentations 4:21–22 and Ezekiel 35; 36:5, Edom is marked out for destruction. In Amos 9:11–12, the text says that Edom will be dispossessed by Israel. The entire book of Obadiah is dedicated to forecasting the destruction of Edom because of how they treated Israel. Psalm 137, arguably the most graphic and vengeful of the imprecatory psalms, is aimed against Edom, calling her the "daughter of Babylon" (vv. 7–8). Finally, in Malachi 1:2–5, the LORD says that he hates Esau and says he will be angry with Edom forever.[35]

Exile; expulsion

Esau abandoned Canaan and founded Edom (Gen 33:16; 36:6–8). The LORD granted him a kingdom and many descendants, but he was, nevertheless, outside of the Promised Land, and from him would come one of Israel's worst enemies, the Amalekites (Gen 36:12). In contrast, Jacob crossed the Jordan River, entered the Promised Land, and purchased land in Shechem (Gen 32:10; 33:18–20), entering it with great wealth (Gen 36:6–7).

34. The judgment may have been postponed due to Esau's fraternal reception of his brother (Gen 33:4).

35. Nevertheless, this does not appear to be a racial rejection of the Edomites, but rather a spiritual one. They are not condemned for their genealogical ancestry, but rather for their spiritual rebellion. Any Edomite who turned to the true God in faith and repentance would be saved (Deut 23:7–8).

Deliverance of righteous remnant

Jacob and his descendants were kept safe, first in Canaan and later in Egypt (Gen 37–50). Their move to Egypt was divinely initiated (Gen 46:3–4), and they were allowed to flourish in peaceful conditions.[36] In fact, Joseph explicitly states that God had sent him to Egypt in order to preserve a remnant for his brothers (Gen 45:7).

As has been seen, God continues to narrow the representative minority through whom he will bless the world. Although the most likely candidate to inherit the Adamic blessing would be Jacob's oldest son, Reuben, he will not be the chosen heir for at least two reasons. First, God has established a pattern of choosing the younger and weaker over the older and stronger, and thus it is not surprising that Reuben is overlooked in the blessing process. Second, Jacob's three oldest sons—Reuben, Simeon, and Levi—have all disqualified themselves as potential heirs by their outrageous public sins of murder and sexual immorality (Gen 34:30; 35:22; cf. 1 Chr 5:1–2).[37] Instead of Jacob blessing these three sons at the end of his life as he does with his other descendants, he curses them (Gen 49:3–7).[38] The next in line to receive the blessing would be Leah's fourth-born son, Judah, or Rachel's first-born son, Joseph (Gen 29:35; 30:24). Not surprisingly, the two sons who received the longest and most important blessings from Jacob were Judah and Joseph (Gen 49:8–12, 22–26), and it is to them that the sons of Jacob will bow down (Gen 37:7–8;

36. It does not seem to be coincidence that seventy Israelites migrated to Egypt (Gen 46:27): as there were seventy nations in Gen 10 with only one being the head of God's line (Eber), now there are seventy heads of Israel with only one being the head of God's line (Perez's son Hezron; Gen 46:12). However, this must be seen as a prophetic headship, since the Judah–Ephraim rivalry is still active and will not be settled for several centuries.

37. By way of passing comment, Reuben's affair with his father's concubine evokes other stories of usurpation through sexual conquest, such as Ham and Absalom.

38. Genesis 49:28 says that Israel blessed his sons, "blessing each with the blessing suitable to him." This appears to be a general statement or something that occurred off the pages of Scripture. Genesis 49:3 may be interpreted as a blessing, but vv. 4–7 appear to be only curses.

42:6; 49:8). Judah will come to represent the tribe of Judah, and Joseph's youngest son Ephraim, who also directly received Jacob's blessing (Gen 48:13–20), will come to represent the tribe of Ephraim. As the biblical story progresses, these two tribes will be the central focus of an ongoing struggle as to which is the true heir of God's blessing, with Judah eventually rising to the top (cf. Num 10:14; Judg 1:2; Ps 78:67–68).[39]

39. Sailhamer, *Pentateuch as Narrative*, 203.

Chapter 4: Moses, Representing the Physical Twelve Tribes of Israel

Exodus–Deuteronomy

Seven generations after Abraham, God recreated with the chosen line of one of the seventy nations, namely, Abraham's line as it was continued through Isaac, Jacob, and the twelve patriarchs. In distinction from previous cycles, this new man that God has chosen was not an individual person, but rather a corporate entity, the nation of Israel. This is one of the most important cycles in the entire biblical story since it coincides with the beginning of Israel's written history and thus becomes the primary salvation event to which others are compared.

1. Creation[1] (Exod 1–15, 25–40)

Creation from chaos

Whereas the patriarchs had managed to survive, even thrive, in Egypt for a brief period, it was short lived, and within a few

1. Cassuto, *Commentary on the Book of Exodus*, 18–19; Gage, *Gospel of Genesis*, 20, 64; Waltke, *Old Testament Theology*, 357; Athas, "The Creation of Israel," 30–59 (esp. 51–57); Morales, *Exodus Old and New*, 48–65. Note also how the early life of Moses foreshadows, models, and/or prefigures several key themes of the Exodus: born as a slave in Egypt in oppression and persecution, undergoes a water ordeal and is delivered, escapes to Midian later in life, and

generations, they had become slaves. God's chosen land was still inhabited by Canaanites, who were filling up their iniquity (Gen 15:16), and God's chosen people had become enslaved by Egyptians (Exod 1:8–14). Thus, the accursed Hamites were overcoming the blessed Shemites. The Israelites were incapable of being a blessing to the rest of creation while they were enslaved to their Egyptian overlords and living outside of God's Promised Land. In fact, it appears as if the Israelites had even forgotten the name of their ancestral God (Exod 3:13–14). Similar to how the builders of Babel had said "Come, let us" and forced others to build a city with bricks and mortar (Gen 11:3–4), so too did Pharaoh say "Come, let us" and forced the Israelites to build the store cities Pithom and Raamses with bricks and mortar (Exod 1:10–14). The Israelites' groaning because of their slavery (Exod 2:23–25) evokes the imagery of the oppressive regimes before the flood and at Babel. What is more, the Egyptians attempted to eradicate the Israelite line by killing the male children (Exod 1:15–22). If they had succeeded, they would have eradicated God's chosen seed through whom he would bless the rest of creation. The Israelites are afflicted and 'cry out' to God (Exod 3:7, 9).[2]

It is within the context of the dark slavery of the Israelites to their Egyptian overlords that God recreated. It should not be surprising, therefore, that creational motifs reappear during Israel's exodus: the separation of light and darkness (Exod 13:21–22; 14:19–20), the division of water (Exod 14:21–22; cf. Ps 78:13), and the emergence of dry land (Exod 14:16, 21–22, 29; cf. Ps 106:9).[3] The 'deep' that was present at creation and the flood is present again as God divides the Red Sea (Exod 15:8; cf. Gen 1:2; 8:2). Isaiah 43 will use the verbs 'create' and 'form' to describe God's creation and formation of Israel, which are the same ones used in Genesis 1–2

sees a theophany of the burning bush at Mount Sinai.

2. Cf. Gen 15:13; Exod 1:11–12; 2:23–24; Num 20:14–16; Deut 26:7; Jos 24:7.

3. Notice as well that the waters are grouped together at the Red Sea as they were at creation (Exod 15:8), and that the 'wind/Spirit' and water are present, again like at creation (Exod 14:21).

to describe God's unique creation of the world and formation of man (Isa 43:1, 7, 15, 21). Indeed, the only thing that Israel's redemption from Egypt can be compared to is creation itself (Deut 4:32). The manna that God will provide for his people in the desert is reminiscent of the mist that watered the land in Eden (Gen 2:6), and it even arrives and disappears with dew (Exod 16:13–21; Num 11:9). As God had 'remembered' Noah in the midst of the flood, once again he 'remembers' his covenant with Abraham, Isaac, and Jacob in the midst of Israel's suffering in Egypt (Exod 2:24).

Creation battle

As the LORD had 'come down' to see the Tower of Babel, so too did he 'come down' to deliver the Israelites from the Egyptians (Exod 3:8). When Moses and Aaron dueled with their Egyptian magician counterparts, Aaron's staff turned into a 'serpent'—the same word used elsewhere in Scripture to refer to the great sea monsters of chaos (Gen 1:21; Isa 27:1; 51:9)—and swallowed the magicians' 'serpent' (Exod 7:8–12).[4] Pharaoh's heart was hardened, and thus God determined to judge Egypt with ten plagues (Exod 7–12). By these ten plagues God was slowly un-creating the false order that the Egyptians had established through violence and oppression and recreating the true order that he wished to establish through the Israelites. This undoing of the creation climaxed in God's sending darkness and death to the Egyptians, thereby evoking the cosmos' pre-creational state of being formless and void (Exod 10:21–11:10; 12:28–30). Although the Egyptians had tried to exterminate the Israelites by throwing their babies into the river, it was God who ended the Egyptian army by casting them into the sea (Exod 1:22; 15:1, 21). As with Noah before, only Moses and the Israelites safely passed through the waters, whereas the Egyptian army was killed by the floodwaters of chaos (Exod 14:13–14, 21–31). In brief, the LORD executed judgment on the Egyptians' gods (Exod 12:12; Num 33:4).

4. This can be seen as a foreshadowing of how the Egyptians will be swallowed up by the Red Sea (Exod 15:12).

After Israel was freed from Egypt and witnessed the destruction of Pharaoh's army, Moses composed a song whose theme was God's battle-victory over Pharaoh (Exod 15:1–18). His "Song of the Sea" abounds with imagery describing God as a victorious warrior who has conquered his foe. Egypt is likened to the primordial sea creature Rahab/Tannin[5] whom God overcomes through the ten plagues and the Red Sea crossing (cf. Exod 14:13–14), thereby evoking how God had overcome primordial chaos with his ten speech acts. The dead bodies of the Egyptian soldiers floating to the seashore evoke the image of a slain sea creature whose corpse has washed ashore (Exod 14:30). As God had 'destroyed' the antediluvian world because of its wickedness, he again sends the 'destroyer' to judge the Egyptians for their wickedness (Exod 12:23).

God's Spirit

As the Spirit had 'hovered' over the waters at creation, once again the Lord 'hovers' over Israel during the Exodus (Deut 32:11; cf. Exod 14:19–20).

God's word

Similar to how God had spoken ten times at creation, now he gives his Ten Words at Mount Sinai (Exod 20; Deut 5; cf. Deut 4:13), by which he created moral order out of the moral chaos of the surrounding nations.[6] This is perhaps the most striking parallel between creational and moral order: Scripture teaches that when mankind rebels against God's moral order, God's creational order rebels against them. Sin and catastrophe are closely connected in Scripture (e.g., Gen 6:5–7).

5. Psalm 87:4; 89:10; Isa 30:7; 51:9–10; Ezek 29:3.

6. Gage, *Gospel of Genesis*, 39 n. 27. The Israelites are commanded repeatedly not to live like their neighbors, but rather to follow God (e.g., Lev 18:3).

Temple

God revealed Moses and the Israelites the tabernacle that they were to construct (Exod 25–31), which later will become the template for the temple.[7] As was alluded to in chapter 1, the material used to build the tabernacle came from what the Israelites requested from the Egyptians (Exod 12:35–36), which could be seen as something similar to victory plunder.

Understanding the tabernacle/temple to be a microcosm of the greater macrocosm of creation has a long history, and modern interest in the topic has uncovered several parallels between the two.[8] While not attempting to be exhaustive, some of the more important linguistic and conceptual items that appear both in Genesis 1–3 and in texts relating to the tabernacle/temple are the following. As God saw his finished work and then blessed it (Gen 1:31–2:3), Moses now sees the finished work of the tabernacle and blesses the people (Exod 39:32, 43; 40:33).[9] As the Spirit had been present in the beginning for the construction of the cosmos-temple, he is present again in Bezalel, empowering him to construct the Israel's tabernacle (Exod 31:1–5; 35:30–33).[10]

7. The tabernacle and temple are essentially identical in function except that the former was mobile while the latter permanent. The two are linked conceptually in Ps 27:4–6.

8. For early discussion, cf. Philo, *Life of Moses*, 2:71–135; *Special Laws*, 1:66–97; *Questions in Exodus*, 2:69–123(ff); Josephus, *Antiq*. 3:179–87; for modern discussion, cf. Wenham, *Genesis 1–15*, 61–86; Beale, *The Temple and the Church's Mission*, 66–80; Keel, *Symbolism*, 112–76; Hinckley, "Adam, Aaron, and the Garden Sanctuary," 5–12; Gage, *Gospel of Genesis*, 39. An additional, potential connection between creation and the tabernacle may be the following: as God had created the world in seven days, he now gives seven speeches in Exod 25–31 which may thematically correspond to the seven days of creation; cf. Kearney, "Creation and Liturgy," 375–78.

9. Key words linking these two texts are "see," "all," "work," "finish," and "bless." The idea of rest (Gen 2:2–3) may also be present in the tabernacle: Moses rested after the completion of the tabernacle, and the ark now had a place of rest (2 Chr 6:41; Ps 132:8).

10. Sailhamer, *Pentateuch as Narrative*, 32. Oholiab may also have been filled with the Spirit in a similar way, as he is mentioned in the same context as Bezalel.

In the Pentateuch, the word 'lights' only appears in two contexts: in Genesis 1:14–16 to refer to the celestial bodies and in speaking of the tabernacle's lampstand.[11] The tree of life in the Garden seems to be evoked by the tree-like golden lampstand used in the tabernacle/temple.[12] The word 'sea' appears in both contexts.[13] 'Gold' appears in both contexts.[14] 'Onyx stone' appears in both contexts.[15] The verbs 'work' and 'keep' appear in both contexts.[16] The complementary words 'nakedness,' 'gird/girdle,' and 'clothe' appear in both contexts.[17] 'Cherubim' appear in both contexts, with an emphasis on guarding the LORD's holiness.[18] God's presence is described as 'walking' in both contexts.[19] Similar to how God would fellowship with Adam and Eve in the 'cool of the day,' the daily sacrifice was offered in the morning and evening (i.e., the

11. Genesis 1:14–16; Exod 25:6; 27:20; Lev 24:2; Num 4:16. Early Jewish commentators drew a connection between the lampstand and the heavenly bodies: Josephus, *Antiq.* 3.14, *War* 5.217; Philo, *Rer. Div. Her.* 221–225, *Vit. Mos.* 2.102-105; *Quaest. Exod.* 2.73-81. Irenaeus stated that the lampstand was a "pattern" after the seven heavens (*Demonstration*, 9).

12. Genesis 2:9; Exod 25:31–36. Josephus speaks of the golden lampstand as decorated with flowers and pomegranates, thereby making it more tree-like (*Antiq.* 3.145).

13. Genesis 1:6–10, 26, 28; 1 Kgs 7:23–26. Othmar Keel writes of the usage of 'sea' in 1 Kgs: "The term 'sea' indicates that this is no mere wash basin (though it naturally fulfilled that function). Rather, its water represents the harnessed, subdued Chaos from which the world arose" (*Symbolism*, 136).

14. Genesis 2:12, Exod 25:11–39; 1 Kgs 6:20–35.

15. Genesis 2:12; Exod 25:7; 28:9–12, 20; 1 Chr 29:2.

16. Genesis 2:15; Num 3:5–8; 8:26; 18:5–6. This combination of verbs is not used elsewhere (but cf. Ps 19:11, which could be seen to extend the priestly role to every man's responsibility through the keeping of Torah).

17. Genesis 3:7, 21; Exod 28:41–42; 29:9; 40:13–14; Lev 21:10. In both contexts, the clothing refers to covering something shameful.

18. Genesis 3:24, Exod 25:18–22; 26:31; 1 Kgs 6:23–35; Ezek 41:18.

19. Genesis 3:8; Lev 26:12; Deut 23:14; 2 Sam 7:6–7. In both contexts, the verb 'walk' appears in the Hiphil stem, which serves to connect the ideas even more closely.

cool of the day).[20] Finally, the entrance to the garden of Eden and the tabernacle/temple was in the east.[21]

Rest

While God's rest is not explicitly stated, its presence is implied in three ways. First, God promises to give rest to Israel (Exod 33:14),[22] which implies his own rest. Second, God filled the tabernacle with his glory, thereby demonstrating his presence with his people, which is emblematic of rest (Exod 40:34–38). Third, the two accounts of the Ten Commandments in Exodus 20 and Deuteronomy 5 speak of rest in the fourth commandment and connect it with the creation and Exodus events (Exod 20:11; Deut 5:15). The implication is that as God rested after creation, he again rests after the Exodus.

2. Man (Exod 1–20)

Election

Whereas in previous cycles an individual had been the covenant mediator, now it is an entire nation, the Israelites (Exod 19:5–6). God referred to them collectively as his firstborn son (Exod 4:22–23; cf. Num 11:12) and made them a kingdom of priests (Exod 19:6). However, God also chose mediators through whom he would deal with the Israelites, such as Moses[23] and the priests, especially Aaron.[24] Moses (and Aaron) was the seventh generation from Abraham and the 26th generation from Adam: it surely is no coincidence that the number 26 is the gematrian

20. Genesis 3:8; Lev 6:8–13.

21. Genesis 3:24; Exod 27:13; Ezek 8:16; 47:1.

22. However, this should not be interpreted as the Israelites having entered into the rest that God had originally intended; cf. Ps 95:7–11 (see below).

23. Exodus 20:18–21; 33:7–11; 34:29–35.

24. As Adam was to work and keep the garden (Gen 2:15), the priests are to keep and guard the tabernacle (e.g., Num 3:7–8). Moses and Aaron are seen as co-deliverers of Israel in 1 Sam 12:8.

equivalent of the LORD's name: YHWH.[25] As God 'saw' that his creation was 'good,' now Moses' mother 'sees' that Moses is 'good' (Exod 2:2). Moses spoke with God face to face and mouth to mouth, as Adam would have done in the garden (Exod 33:11; Num 12:6–8). As in previous cycles, Moses' occupation—as well as that of his father-in-law Jethro[26]—was shepherding, and thus he had the ideal experience to nurture God's people physically and spiritually (Exod 2:16–22; 3:1).

There are also many factors that suggest Moses was a kind of second Noah: Noah made an 'ark' and Moses was placed in an 'ark' (Exod 2:3, 5),[27] and both were sealed in a similar fashion.[28] Both figures were messengers of death for God's enemies and of life for God's people. Both figures led their people through the waters of death. Similar to how the end of the flood was on the first day of the first month of a new year (Gen 8:13), so too was the tabernacle erected on the first day of the first month of a new year (Exod 40:17), as if to suggest a parallel between creational order and religious order.[29]

Formed outside; 'go forth'

Israel 'went forth' from Egypt (e.g., Exod 12:17, 41–42, 51; Deut 26:8), was formed in the desert, and entered the Promised Land, first in the land east of the Jordan River and then into the Promised Land itself (see below).

25. Sasson, "A Genealogical 'Convention,'" 12 n. 2 (cf. Sasson, "The 'Tower of Babel,'" 214 n. 7).

26. Jethro's other name, Reuel (Num 10:29), could mean either "friend of God" or "shepherd of God."

27. The word 'ark' is only mentioned in Gen 6–9 and Exod 2:3, 5. Surely this cannot be mere coincidence.

28. Genesis 6:14; Exod 2:3.

29. After surveying similar parallels between Noah and Moses, Dale Allison writes, "One can hardly avoid the thought that Moses was a second Noah" (*New Moses*, 203).

Mixed multitude

As Abraham had come out of Babylon with Lot,[30] now Israel comes out of Egypt as a 'mixed' multitude (Exod 12:38), probably including both Egyptians and Israelites who were not truly Israelites in their hearts (cf. Rom 9:6; Heb 3:7–19). This mixture will prove fatal for the Israelites and will lead to their wilderness wanderings.

Mountain and garden

God met with Israel on the mountain of God (Exod 18:5), otherwise known as Horeb or Mount Sinai (e.g., Exod 19:1; 33:6), and the entire middle portion of the Pentateuch relates this encounter (Exod 19:1–Num 10:10). The tabernacle was constructed so as to evoke various garden features (Exod 25–27; 30), and its purpose was to restore fellowship—albeit limited—between God and his people (Exod 25:8; 29:45–46).[31] Interestingly, the mountain and garden features come together in a striking way in Exodus 15:17, where Moses says that God will plant Israel on his own mountain. Similarly, Isaiah 5:1–2 describes the formation of Israel as creating a vineyard on a mountain slope, which poetically brings together the ideas of mountain and garden. At times, the Israelites are even described with garden-like imagery (e.g., Num 24:5–6). As God's presence with Adam and Eve had been described as a walking voice, again there is a walking voice as God met with Israel to give them his law (Exod 19:19).

30. Sailhamer argues that in Gen 12:10–13:4, Lot occupies the same position as the "mixed multitude" of Exod 12:38 (*Pentateuch as Narrative*, 38).

31. Although more speculative, Exod 24:9–11 briefly recounts the story of Moses, the priests, and seventy elders going up the mountain, beholding God, and eating and drinking in his presence. This obviously evokes the covenant theme, but it may also allude to the garden theme. It could be argued that fellowship with God—the emblem of which is sharing a meal with him—is the ultimate goal of humanity, something not too dissimilar from eating from the Tree of Life (cf. Matt 26:29 *pars*). This understanding would further link their meal with the garden motif. Eating is also the essence of a covenant, and the meal may be the ratification of the covenant between God and man.

Divine blessing and commands

Israel was blessed by God (Num 22:12; 24:9) and they were 'fruitful' and 'multiplied' (Gen 47:27) and became great, mighty, and numerous (Deut 26:5). Exodus 1:7 is especially important, since all five verbs repeat and evoke the language and imagery of Genesis 1:28 and 9:7: they were 'fruitful,' 'increased greatly' (lit: 'swarmed'), 'multiplied,' 'became strong,' and 'filled' the land (cf. Ps 105:23–24).[32]

While at Mount Sinai, God gave the Israelites foundational teaching and laws, such as the Ten Words, sacrifices, impurity regulations, etc. This is known as the Mosaic covenant (e.g., Exod 24:7–8).[33] However, at least three differences with other covenants ought to be noted. First, Israel's blessing and cursing is tied to their obedience (Lev 26; Deut 27–28). While this is true of all the covenants in a limited way, the connection is especially prominent in the Mosaic covenant. Second, the Mosaic covenant was a temporary covenant that expired with the coming of Abraham's promised seed (Gal 3:17–19) and had the purpose of demonstrating Israel's sinfulness (Gal 3:19). Third, Moses is the only covenant mediator that is not found in the Messianic genealogy.[34]

32. Speaking from the context of Exod 1:7, Terrence Freitheim writes, "Verse 7 connects not only with historical promises [made with the patriarchs] but also with the creation/recreation accounts of Gen. 1:28 and 9:1, 7. . . . The point here is that *God's intentions in creation are being realized in this family*; what is happening is in tune with God's creational purposes. This is *a microcosmic fulfillment of God's macrocosmic design* for the world. . . . These growth passages are *testimony to God's ongoing work of creation and blessing*" (*Exodus*, 25 [italics original]). For more references that apply similar language to the Israelites, cf. Exod 1:12; 5:5; 32:13; Lev 26:9; Deut 1:10–11; 6:3; 7:12–14; 30:5, 16; Neh 9:23; Ps 105:24.

33. Israel is promised that if they keep God's law they will live long in the Promised Land (e.g., Deut 4:40; 5:16, 33; 6:2; 11:8–9, 20–21; 30:20; 32:46–47), which is reminiscent of God's promise to Adam in the garden. However, as Adam's sin led him to exile and death, Israel's sin leads them to exile and death (e.g., Deut 4:25–28; 8:19–20; 11:16–17; 30:18; Josh 23:16).

34. There is no doubt that the Mosaic covenant was a covenant (Deut 29:25; Judg 2:1; 1 Kgs 8:9, 21; 2 Chr 5:10; Jer 31:32; 34:13; Hag 2:5). However, as Gage writes, "Moses is not a covenant of promise. The genealogy of Christ, the promised Seed, is traceable through every covenantal administration but

Moses was a Levite, and the Messiah was to come from the tribe of Judah (Gen 49:8–12). Similar to others before him, Moses was a prophet (Deut 18:15; 34:10), priest (Exod 33:7–11; Ps 99:6), and king (Exod 18:13; cf. Exod 2:14).

3. Fall (Exod 32; Num 13–14; or several texts from Exod 15–32 and Num 11–25)

While in previous cycles it has been relatively easy to identify one particular sin that was committed by God's chosen man and by which he proved himself unworthy to be God's mediator, this is not the case here. Rather, there seem to be three options, each of which exhibit several themes typically associated with the fall stage (see *Excursus* at the end of this chapter for the option that I prefer).

Option 1: the Golden Calf (Exod 32)

First, it could be that the fall occurred at Mount Sinai with the making of the golden calf (Exod 32:1–29).[35] In this scenario, the original garden temptation was essentially reenacted.[36] God had just reminded the Israelites to keep his sabbaths (Exod 31:12–17), but instead they chose to rebel. Aaron, instead of remaining vigilant on the mountain (Exod 24:12–14), went down to the people who tempted him to rebel against God and gave into the temptation with almost no hesitation (Exod 32:1–4).[37] They celebrated

---

Moses. Consequently the Old Covenant stands very much alongside the redemptive program covenantally furthered through Adam, Noah, Abraham, and David" (*Gospel of Genesis*, 36).

35. This was considered by many ancient Jews and Christians as the worst sin that Israel ever committed; cf. Smolar and Aberbach, "The Golden Calf Episode." After reviewing the evidence, the authors conclude, "To all intents and purposes, the calf cult was considered the worst sin ever committed by Israel . . . one that had left a permanent mark in Jewish history" (106).

36. Carmichael, *The Sacrificial Laws of Leviticus*, 24–27. Carmichael introduces the parallels with this statement: "The narrator of the Primary History views the construction of the calf as a real-life recurrence of happenings in the Adam and Eve story."

37. Perhaps there is significance in the Israelites taking off their own

their rebellion with eating, drinking, and shameful nakedness (Exod 32:6). After Moses had come down from the mountain, they all became aware of their sin, and like Adam, Aaron sought to shift the blame away from himself and toward others (Exod 32:19, 21–24). Like the serpent, the Israelites were forced to eat dust when they consumed the golden calf which had been ground up into powder (Exod 32:20). Some died the very day that the sin occurred (Exod 32:25–28, 35), but by God's merciful forgiveness they were not entirely consumed (Exod 32:9–14).[38] They were threatened with the curse of the loss of God's presence (Exod 33:1–3), but finally forgiven and assured of God's presence (Exod 33:14–17). Also notable is the fact that God said the Israelites had 'corrupted' or 'destroyed' themselves, thereby evoking his earlier evaluation of the pre-flood generation (Exod 32:7; cf. Gen 6:11–13, 17; Ps 106:23).[39]

Option 2: Refusal to enter Canaan (Num 13–14)

Second, it could be that the fall occurred in the wilderness of Paran when the Israelites sent twelve spies into Canaan and, upon hearing their report, refused to enter (Num 13–14).[40] In this scenario,

jewelry, such as evoking Adam and Eve surrendering their pre-fall glory (Ps 106:20 may suggest this connection). Also, notice how Aaron 'formed' the golden calf (Exod 32:4), very similar to how God had 'formed' mankind and the garden of Eden (Gen 2:7–8, 19), thereby making Aaron a kind of anti-God. Also, their turning aside "quickly" (Exod 32:8) fits the implied narrative of the garden of Eden, that it did not take long for Adam and Eve to eat the fruit.

38. Instead, Moses atoned for their sins (Exod 32:30; cf. Ps 106:23), which evokes the sacrificial animal of the garden of Eden (Gen 3:21). Had God destroyed Israel and recreated a new nation through Moses (Exod 32:7–10), this would have broken the promised seed line, which, in this point of the narrative, has been promised to Joseph (Ephraim) or Judah.

39. Another way of looking at this story through the lens of Adam and Eve's fall would be to see Moses as a new Adam, Aaron as a new Eve, and the people as a new serpent: while Moses is absent, Aaron is seduced by the people to abandon God.

40. Dennis Olson refers to the spy story as the "climactic rebellion" of the first half of the book, chapters 1–25 (*Numbers*, 4). While his overall division of the book into chapters 1–25 and 26–36 may need a slight revision (esp. with

Israel's lack of vigilance was demonstrated by their lack of faith in rejecting the godly counsel of Joshua and Caleb, listening instead to the deceptive counsel of the other spies (Num 13:25–33), and attempting to usurp Moses' leadership and take the Israelites back to Egypt (Num 14:1–4). As God had appeared in the garden and at Babel before bringing judgment, here his glory appeared in the tabernacle before bringing judgment (Num 14:10; cf. Exod 16:10). It is significant that it is in the context of this sin that God said that Israel had tested him ten times (Num 14:22), which could suggest that it functioned as a kind of climactic rebellion of the wilderness generation that left Egypt.[41] After Moses reported to the Israelites the LORD's words of punishment (Num 14:26–35), they became aware of their sin and were grieved by it (Num 14:39), and some even tried to cover up their own sin by advancing without God's blessing (Num 14:40–45), the results of which were as ineffectual as Adam and Eve's attempt to cover themselves with fig leaves. God punished the Israelites for their sin with death for all who were twenty years and older and forty years of wandering in the wilderness (Num 14:21–23, 26–38),[42] and refused to allow the older generation of Israelites to enter his rest (Num 14:23; Ps 95:11; cf. Heb 3:7–4:11). In fact, God was even angry with Moses on this occasion, and because of this sin, Moses was not allowed to enter the Promised Land (Deut 1:34–40). Nevertheless, God forgave his people (Num 14:20). In the end, only Caleb was blessed for his obedience (Num 14:24).

respect to chapters 1–10), the point remains that chapters 13–14 are pivotal to understanding the first half of Num.

41. In Num 32:14, whether the syntax refers to the first or second generation, the point is that all who refused to enter into the Promised Land belonged to the "brood of sinful men."

42. This evokes Cain's story: as Cain was supposed to rule over sin (Gen 4:7), the Israelites were supposed to rule over many nations (Deut 15:6); but as Cain wandered for his disobedience (Gen 4:12, 16), the Israelites wandered in the wilderness for their disobedience (Num 14:33–34).

Option 3: General Rebellion

Third, it could be that there was not one particular sin, but rather several which, when taken as a whole, point to the overall rebellious nature of the Israelites (e.g., Num 14:19).[43] This possibility becomes more plausible when it is noticed that the Bible relates ten communal[44] sins of the Israelites during their desert period (cf. Num 14:22), as if to suggest that just as God had created the Israelites through the Ten Words, the Israelites have uncreated themselves through ten communal acts of disobedience, similar to what God had done to Egypt through the ten plagues.[45] There are different ways to tabulate these sins, but according to one reading the sins were as follows: Exodus 15:22–27 (Marah); 16:1–20 (manna and quail); 17:1–7 (Massah/Meribah); 32:1–29 (golden calf); Numbers 11 (Tarebah and Kibroth-hattaavah); 14 (Canaan spies); 16–17 (Korah, Dathan, and Abiram; budding of Aaron's rod); 20:1–13 (Meribah of Kadesh; cf. Num 27:14); 21:4–9 (fiery serpents); 25 (Baal of Peor).[46]

Whatever the case may be, by the time Israel was ready to enter the Promised Land, they were already marked as an unrighteous

43. The justification for this view would be based loosely on the precedence of God's collective blessing and commands given to the patriarchs, for example.

44. Individual or private sins include Lev 10:1–7 (Nadab and Abihu), Num 12 (Miriam and Aaron), and Num 22:22 (Balaam).

45. This is not to say that they broke each individual commandment with each of these rebellions, but rather that, when taken as a whole, they had been equally as rebellious as the obedience to which God had called them in the Ten Words.

46. Deuteronomy 9 and Ps 106 recount several such rebellions, and in Num 14:22 God tells Moses that the Israelites had tested him ten times. *ARN* §34 lists ten trials by which Israel put God to the test in the wilderness. Although my list differs slightly from the one given in *ARN*, the point remains that Israel sinned ten times. It should be noted that the number ten often is used as a round number and need not be interpreted literally (e.g., Gen 31:7, 41; Job 19:3). The point, however, is that the number ten signifies completeness. For a different tabulation of the ten testings, cf. Winnett, *The Mosaic Tradition*, 121–54 (he lists the following texts: Exod 14:11ff; 15:24; 16:2ff; 17:2ff; Num 11:1, 4–6; 14:1–4; 16:12–14; 20:2–5; 21:5).

and stiff-necked people, only slightly more righteous than the nations they were going to dispossess (Deut 9:4–5). In fact, several texts state that Israel had begun to sin from the moment they left Egypt.[47] According to a later biblical writer, this generation of Israelites had rebelled, disobeyed, and sinned because at a fundamental level they did not believe in God (Heb 3:12–19). In summary, Israel did not remain vigilant in guarding against the intrusion of evil, but rather fell into sin like their predecessors had done.

4. Division (Num 13–25)

Division

Throughout Israel's desert experience, there was a clear division between those who wanted to forsake God and return to Egypt, and those who did not.[48] As the books of Exodus and Numbers imply, it was the older generation—described as men of war (Deut 2:14–16; Josh 5:4, 6)[49]—who grumbled, disbelieved, and wanted to return to Egypt (Num 14:26–30; cf. 1 Cor 10:5–6; Jude 5). The older, faithless generation—who did not even circumcise their children (Josh 5:2–7)—presented a continual threat to the younger, believing generation to turn away from following God. The older generation represented rebellion, whereas the younger generation represented hope, and looked forward to God's future blessing.[50]

This division between the believing and unbelieving Israelites is seen already in the story of the twelve spies. They were all chosen as heads from the twelve tribes, and thus represented all Israel (Num 13:2–3). Ten of the spies—representing the unbelieving Israelites—refused to enter Canaan, and only the Judahite Caleb and Ephraimite Joshua—representing the believing Israelites—encouraged them to trust the Lord and take the land (Num 14:6–9).

47. For example, Num 14:19; Deut 31:27; Josh 24:14; 1 Sam 8:7–8; Ps 106:6–7; Ezek 20:4–8.

48. Exodus 16:3; 17:3; 32:1–4; Num 11:4–6; 14:2–4; 20:2–5; 21:4–5.

49. This is somewhat of an ironic description of this generation, since "war" is precisely what they should have made with the Canaanites, but they refused.

50. Olson, *Numbers*, 3–7.

As the biblical story progresses, Judah and Ephraim come to represent believing Israel, and the other tribes come to represent unbelieving Israel (until, of course, Ephraim also becomes associated with unbelieving Israel, thus leaving only Judah).

Persecution

As Israel continued its wilderness wanderings, they had disputes and skirmishes with the Edomites (Num 20:14–21), Canaanites (Num 21:1–3), Amorites (Num 21:21–32), and Bashanites (Num 21:33–35). The Moabites tried to call down curses on the Israelites, but they failed (Num 22–24).

Cities

Many of the places (= cities) that were 'named' during Israel's desert experience were the result of their disobedience and of God's punishment (Exod 15:23; 17:7; Num 11:3, 34; 13:24).[51]

Apostasy; inter-marriage

Although previous attempts to persecute the Israelites had failed, Balak and the Moabites succeeded in luring them into apostasy through sexual immorality (Num 25:1; cf. Rev 2:14). Israelite men fornicated with Moabite women and worshipped Baal of Peor (Num 25:1–8). As a result, God sent a plague that killed 24,000 people (Num 25:9; 31:16).

Prophet; preacher of righteousness

Moses was the major, or perhaps only, prophet/preacher of righteousness that the Israelites had, and often they did not heed his voice.

51. A notable exception is Num 21:3, but "destruction" is not a particularly beautiful name.

Affliction; 'crying out'.

Moses repeatedly 'cried out' to the LORD for help and deliverance (Exod 15:25; 17:4; Num 12:13).

5. Judgment (Num 14–25)

Chaos; flood

As creation originally had been 'formless,' Israel's wanderings took place in a 'wasteland' (Deut 32:10).[52] As God had sent 'plagues' on the Egyptians, now he kills the older generation with 'plagues' (Num 14:37; 16:48–50; 25:8–9).

Exile; expulsion

By the end of Israel's forty-year wanderings in the wilderness, nearly the entirety of the Exodus generation had been killed for their sin: all those over the age of twenty had died (Deut 2:14–16), as had Aaron, Miriam, and Moses (Num 20:1, 22–29; Deut 34:1–8).

Deliverance of righteous remnant

Only the righteous remnant of Joshua, Caleb, and the younger generation were delivered from the wilderness wanderings and will be able to enter the Promised Land.

52. These are the only two uses of this word in the Pentateuch.

Excursus: The Fall in the Exodus Cycle

DESPITE THE STRENGTHS OF the first (golden calf) and third (ten communal sins) options explained above, I slightly favor the second (twelve spies) option for the following eight reasons.[1] First, Numbers 13–14 is one of the longest narrative sections in the book of Numbers, which suggests its relative importance: it gives the book its unifying theme—the transition from the Exodus generation to the new generation that enters the Promised Land—as well as its unifying structure—it provides the link between the two censuses in Numbers 1 (the old generation) and 26 (the new generation).[2] Second, Numbers 13–14 is preceded by three rebellions that become progressively worse: the first affected the fringe of the camp (Num 11:1–3), the second involved common people (Num 11:4–35), and the third involved the leaders Miriam and Aaron (Num 12:1–6). Thus, Israel's refusal to enter the land—a decision made by all Israel (Num 13:2; 14:1–2)—can be seen as the

1. Olson, *Numbers*, 75–90; Condie, "Narrative Features of Numbers 13–14," 124–25. Philip Budd argues that Num 13–14 is "archetypal" for the theme of dispossession, that it is the center of a chiastic structure of "stories of disaffection from Sinai to the Jordan," and that it "occupies a central place" in the narrative (*Numbers*, 162–63).

2. Numbers 14:29 uses the same formula used in Num 1:3, 18, etc., and Num 26:63–65 explicitly evokes the spy story.

climax of Israel's disobedience, the moment in which the people as a whole rebelled against God. Third, for the first time in Israel's desert wanderings, the people not only murmur and complain, but even plan to rebel against God, and in a very significant way: they plan to return to Egypt (Num 14:4). In short, they are attempting to reverse the Exodus, that is, to undo the new creation that God is bringing about. Fourth, the punishment meted out here—death for everyone over the age of 20—is unlike that of other punishments that Israel had received to this point. Even after the sin with the golden calf in Exodus 32, only a relatively limited number of people were killed (Exod 32:25–28, 35); nothing like the huge numbers involved here. Fifth, this episode is thematically related to the beginning of Numbers, which itself is connected to the Exodus: in Numbers 1–10, Israel was being prepared for battle and to enter the Promised Land, but in Numbers 13–14 they failed to go to battle and enter the land. Sixth, of all Israel's wilderness sins, Moses mentioned this one in the historical prologue section of Deuteronomy, and it was because of their rebellion here that, at least in part, he too was denied entrance into the Promised Land (Deut 1:19–45).[3] Seventh, the entire biblical narrative from at least the Exodus, if not as early as the patriarchal narratives or earlier, has been anticipating this moment: when Abraham's descendants finally possess the Promised Land. This makes the Israelite rebellion of special significance: it was an emphatic, national "No!" to God's plan. Eighth, Numbers 13–14 is followed with a division between the older and younger generations (see above), with godly Joshua and Caleb representing the tribes of Ephraim and Judah, respectively (Num 13:6, 8, 16). This division pushes the biblical story along and narrows the representative(s) with whom God will work to bless the world.

3. Numbers 20:10–12 provides another reason: Moses' disobedience in striking the rock (cf. Num 27:12–14; Deut 9:7–21).

Chapter 5: Joshua, Representing the Spiritual Twelve Tribes of Israel

Joshua–1 Samuel

TEN GENERATIONS AFTER ABRAHAM, and after ten testings in the wilderness, God recreated again through Joshua.[1] Of the physical, chosen descendants of Abraham, only Joshua (Ephraim) and Caleb (Judah) trusted in God and were willing to enter the Promised Land. This cycle is unique from previous cycles, in that God will not establish a new covenant with Joshua, but rather confirm a previous covenant (Mosaic) with him. Similar to the previous cycle, God is working with a people, the nation of Israel, but now it is a nation that has been purified of its Egyptian corruptions. The geographic focus has reduced again, from the land between the Euphrates and Nile rivers to its central section: Canaan.

1. Creation (Josh 1–24)

Creation from chaos

Although the Israelites had conquered some land on the east side of the Jordan River, they remained on the plains of Moab (Deut 34:5–8), and thus there was a sense in which they were still outside of the Promised Land. In addition, they had been left to

1. See Appendix IV for this calculation.

mourn the death of their leader, Moses (Deut 34:7–8). They have yet to enter the 'rest' that God promised them (Deut 12:9; 25:19). Some of Moses' final words—and some of the LORD's final words to and through Moses—warned Israel of future apostasy and exile (Deut 31:14–29). Thus, although anticipation was present, the atmosphere was one of sobriety and darkness. It was in this context that the conquest of Canaan began.

Many parallels with the Exodus, but also with creation, can be seen. As God had divided the waters at creation, and as Moses had divided the waters at the Red Sea to lead Israel out of Egypt, here again Joshua divides the waters at the Jordan River to lead Israel into the Promised Land (Jos 3–4).[2] As the waters had stood in a heap when Israel crossed the Red Sea, here again they stand in a heap when they cross the Jordan (Josh 3:13, 16; cf. Exod 15:8). As Hebrew children were to ask their parents about the meaning of Passover, now they are to ask their parents about the meaning of the twelve stones in the Jordan River.[3] Joshua 4:23 and Psalm 114:3 explicitly connect the Red Sea and Jordan crossings: the latter was a re-doing of the former. As God had delivered Israel from Egypt with 'wonders' (Exod 3:20), here again God divided the Jordan River with 'wonders' (Josh 3:5). Some have even argued that the structure of the book of Joshua reflects God's process of creation: as God created order and structural spaces on days 1–3, filled the spaces on days 4–6, and then rested on day 7, similarly Joshua conqueres the land and creates space for the Israelites to live (Josh 1–12), fills it with the life of the Israelites (Josh 13–21), and confirms the covenant that inaugurates their rest (Josh 22–24).[4]

2. Although the word for the division of waters is different in Josh 3:13 than the one used in Gen 1:6–10, the imagery is nevertheless evoked. The word for the dry ground on which they cross (Josh 3:17) is different than the one used to speak of Moses and the Israelites' crossing (e.g., Exod 14:16), but will be used again later to speak of Elijah's parting of the same river (2 Kgs 2:8).

3. Joshua 4:6–7, 21–23; cf. Exod 12:26–27; Deut 6:20–25.

4. Waltke, *Old Testament Theology*, 513.

Creation battle

According to the list given in Genesis 15:18–21, ten groups of Canaanites were living in the Promised Land.[5] Giants, the descendants of Anak and of the antediluvian Nephilim, were living in Canaan in fortified cities with high walls (e.g., Num 13:28–29, 32–33; Deut 1:28), a seemingly insurmountable obstacle for God's people. Yet as the first battle at Jericho demonstrated, God himself was fighting for Israel, and thus their enemies were no match (Josh 6). This battle, illustrative of the entire campaign, was decisive: except for the household of Rahab and some precious metal that was later put in the treasury of the LORD's house, the entire city, including everything and everyone in it, was destroyed (Josh 6:20–25).[6] Similar to how Adam and Eve had been 'driven' from the garden of Eden after their sin, the Canaanites were 'driven' from the Promised Land because of their sin (Josh 24:12, 18; cf. Gen 15:16).[7] As creation battles in previous cycles had spoken of God defeating the great sea monsters, this cycle speaks of God defeating the great land giants.

God's Spirit

As Moses had encountered the LORD at the burning bush in Sinai (Exod 3:1–6), so too did Joshua encounter the LORD, referred to as the "commander of the army of the LORD" (Josh 5:13–15). God's Spirit dwelt in Joshua (Num 27:18), and God promised to be with him and the Israelites wherever they went (Deut 31:6,

5. The number varies in different texts, usually between five and seven, but the first time they are mentioned in Gen 15, the number is ten.

6. As the flood had destroyed everything that had the breath of life (Gen 6:17; 7:22), everything was destroyed in Canaan that had the breath of life (Josh 6:21; 10:40; 11:11, 14; cf. Deut 20:17); cf. Gage, *Gospel of Genesis*, 65. This was the "ban" (Heb: חֵרֶם, *herem*).

7. It is interesting to note that the word "Canaanite" may come from the Hebrew verb כנע (*cana'*) meaning "submission" or "humiliation." If this is correct, then the very name of the Canaanites implies their destiny to be submitted to the Israelites who are to 'subdue' and 'have dominion' over them (Postell, *Adam as Israel*, 105–06).

8, 23; Josh 1:5, 9). As God's Spirit had accompanied Moses and Israel in the desert, he now accompanies Joshua and Israel (Num 27:18; Deut 34:9).

God's word

As God had spoken ten times to Abraham, Isaac, and Jacob to create his new people, he again speaks to Joshua on ten separate occasions to bring his people into the Promised Land.[8]

Temple

After the Conquest, Israel set up the tabernacle in Shiloh (Josh 18:1), which was in obedience to Moses' words given in Deuteronomy 12. It is here, in the presence of the LORD at Shiloh, that the leaders of Israel divide up the land according to lot (Josh 19:51). Shiloh is where the tabernacle will remain until God chooses Jerusalem as his dwelling place (e.g., 1 Sam 1:3; Ps 78:60). Near the end of his life, Joshua set up a kind of open-air sanctuary at Shechem (Josh 24:26).[9]

Rest

Israel was charged to enter the Promised Land because God wanted to give them 'rest' (Josh 1:13, 15), and after the Conquest was

8. The exact phrase "And the LORD said to Joshua" occurs 12 times in the book of Joshua: 1:1; 3:7; 4:1, 15; 5:2, 9; 6:2; 7:10; 8:1, 18; 10:8; 11:6. However, on three occasions, God speaks to Joshua during the same event, reducing the number to nine (4:1 and 15; 5:2 and 9; 8:1 and 18), and in Jos 13:1, a near-exact phrase occurs, "And the LORD said to him [Joshua]," functioning as the final time the LORD speaks to Joshua as part of bringing his people into the Promised Land.

9. Bethel and Shiloh were located in the mountainous region belonging to Ephraim, and Shechem in the mountainous region of Manasseh. Thus, with three holy sites within the region given to Joseph's descendants, it would seem as if the chosen line would flow through him, and especially Ephraim. Nevertheless, when God chooses Jerusalem, which is located within the borders of the southern kingdom of Judah, God's intentions will be made clear. Perhaps this is yet another example of God choosing the lesser over the greater.

complete, God is said to have given them 'rest' in fulfillment of the promises that he had made to the patriarchs (Josh 21:44; 22:4; 23:1; cf. 11:23; 14:15[10]).

2. Man (Josh 1–24)

Election

As God had made a covenant with Israel at Mount Sinai, here Israel reaffirms that relationship during the covenant renewal ceremony at Mount Ebal and Mount Gerazim (Josh 8:30–35). As Moses had acted as the key mediator before, now that role has been passed on to Joshua, who was commissioned publicly by Moses in the tent of meeting in the presence of the Lord (Num 27:18–23; Deut 31:1–8, 14–15, 23). Now Israel stands in awe of Joshua as they had done previously with Moses (Josh 4:14), and Joshua's leadership is compared to a shepherd taking care of his sheep (Num 27:17). As with his predecessors, Joshua is portrayed as a prophet (e.g., Josh 24:2), priest (e.g., Josh 8:30–35), and king (e.g., Josh 23:2).

Formed outside; 'go forth'

The Israelites had been formed during their forty years of desert wanderings, and all the males were circumcised before the Conquest began (Josh 5:2–7). All were reminded that they had 'gone forth' out of Egypt (Josh 2:10; 24:5–6).

Mixed multitude

Nevertheless, Israel was still not pure, and there was sin during (and after) the conquest. Men like Achan demonstrate that even the younger generation was not entirely holy (see below).

10. The verbs used in Josh 11:23 and 14:15 are different, but the general point is the same: God's rest is present.

Mountain and garden

Joshua's commissioning happened at Mount Nebo in the Abarim mountain range (cf. Deut 32:49),[11] where he was appointed Moses' successor and leader of Israel (Num 27:12–23). Not to be forgotten are the numerous references that describe the Promised Land with garden imagery, at times even evoking Eden itself.[12] After the conquest, the tabernacle was set up in the mountainous region of Shiloh, thereby evoking the man–mountain–garden complex once again.[13] Joshua's covenant ceremony took place in the mountain region of Shechem under a terebinth tree, again evoking the idea of an open-air temple (Josh 24:25–26).

Divine blessing and commands

The Israelites received God's blessings throughout the Conquest period (Josh 8:33; 22:6). As they entered the Promised Land, they were very numerous (Deut 1:10–11; Neh 9:23). With Joshua as their leader, the Israelites were commanded to conquer Canaan (Josh 1:1–9), and they were able, in part, to 'subdue' the land (Josh 18:1; cf. Josh 1:3; 13:1–7; Neh 9:24), which is remarkable since this is the first significant use of the verb 'subdue' since Genesis 1:28.[14]

11. The biblical texts are ambiguous regarding Joshua's position on the mountain. The book of Deut is set within the context of the "plains" and "land" of Moab (Num 36:13; Deut 29:1; 34:1), but for a public commissioning to be visible and audible to the people, it seems reasonable to assume that he would be on a higher elevation than merely at the foot of the mountain (although not on the mountain top either; cf. Deut 32:49; 34:1).

12. Genesis 13:10; Exod 3:8; Num 13:17–29; 14:7–8; Deut 1:25; 6:10–11; 8:7–10; 11:11–12; Josh 24:13; Jer 2:7; Ezek 20:6, 15; Neh 9:25. Significantly, in Lev 26:1–13 and Deut 7:12–16; 28, God promised that, if the Israelites kept his covenant, he would make the Promised Land flourish in a manner reminiscent of paradise. That is to say, the re-flourishing of Eden was based on the Israelites' faithfulness to the covenant.

13. Joshua 18:1; Judg 18:31; 21:19; 1 Sam 1:3, 24; 2:14; 4:3–4; 14:3; 1 Kgs 14:2; Ps 78:60. The mountainous region of Gibeon was also a holy site (1 Kgs 3:4–5; 1 Chr 16:39; 21:29; 2 Chr 1:3, 13).

14. The two other uses before Josh 18:1 are Num 32:22 and 29, which anticipate the Conquest.

Pockets of resistance remained, but the Canaanites's power to resist the Israelites had been broken. No mention is made of a covenant with Joshua, but it is significant that Deuteronomy 29:1 mentions another covenant that the LORD made with Israel besides the one he had made with them earlier at Mount Sinai, and that God commanded Joshua to be faithful to the Mosaic covenant (Josh 1:1–8), which Joshua later renewed with the people both during and after the Conquest (Josh 8:30–35; 23–24). Additionally, it is significant that Joshua mediated another covenant between the LORD and the Israelites at Shechem (Josh 24:25–28).

3. Fall (Josh 7; 9; Judg)

As with the Israelites in their desert wanderings, there does not appear to have been one definitive sin that caused the younger generation to fall. Rather, it seems that there were two sins: one committed by an individual Israelite (which nevertheless had consequences for the whole community), and one committed by Joshua and the Israelite community. Both have clear verbal and thematic allusions to Adam and Eve's sin, and thus both are presented below.

The first major turning point in the conquest narrative comes in Joshua 7 with Achan's violation of the ban (Josh 7:1).

Not vigilant

Instead of being vigilant and waiting for the LORD to give instruction, Joshua and Israel rushed into battle against Ai (Josh 7:2–3). Joshua was just as irresponsible in listening to the advice of the people as Adam had been in listening to Eve, and as Aaron had been in listening to the people.

Woman; deception/seduction; usurpation

The Israelites deceived themselves into thinking that they could win battles—especially against Ai, a town whose name means "ruin"—without the LORD's blessing (Josh 7:1). As Eve had attempted to win, but ultimately lost, an intellectual battle on her own against the innocuous serpent, Israel tried to win, but ultimately lost, a physical battle on their own against the innocuous town of Ai. The Israelites had 'broken faith,' which is a very strong verb normally reserved to describe marital infidelity and blatant sin against the LORD (Josh 7:1; cf. Num 5:6; 2 Chr 28:19). For the moment, it appeared that the Canaanites had usurped Israel's ability to live in the Promised Land, and Israel feared that they had been completely overthrown (Josh 7:4–9).

Knowledge of sin

Achan's sin is described in terms that have numerous linguistic parallels with Eve's sin in Genesis 3:6: he 'saw' a 'good' cloak and other plunder, and 'desired' and 'took' them (Josh 7:21); he then attempted to "hide" what he had done but was ashamed when found out and confessed where the spoils were to be found.

Curse

Reminiscent of the death threat found in Genesis 2:16–17, Achan and his family died the very day that their sin was discovered (Josh 7:24–26).[15]

Forgiveness

After the sin had been taken care of, God forgave Israel (Josh 7:26).

The second major turning point, and one which foreshadows the reason for Israel's future apostasy, comes in Joshua 9 with Israel's treaty with the Gibeonites.

15. It is surely more than mere coincidence that 3,000 people were killed as punishment for the golden calf episode and 3,000 soldiers fled in battle as punishment for Achan's sin (Exod 32:28; Josh 7:4–5).

Not vigilant

While Joshua and the Israelites put on a show of due diligence with respect to their visitors (Josh 9:7–8), they did not consult the LORD before acting (Josh 9:14–15), much like Eve failed to do.

Woman; deception/seduction; usurpation

Instead, the Gibeonites, who are described as acting with 'cunning' (Josh 9:4; cf. Gen 3:1), deceived the Israelites into making a treaty with them (Josh 9:15). It is as if the Gibeonites were asking, "Did God really say . . . ?" By making a treaty, the Gibeonites had effectively usurped the Israelites' right to inherit four towns in the Promised Land (Josh 9:16–18).[16]

Knowledge of sin

When they became aware of the truth, some Israelites wanted to attack the town in an attempt to cover their guilt (Josh 9:18b–19), but this was an impossibility since the LORD would have become angry with them (Josh 9:20).

Curse

As the serpent in the garden had been 'cursed' to slither on his belly and as Canaan had been 'cursed' to be a servant of servants to his brothers, so too were the Gibeonites 'cursed' and relegated to woodcutters and water carriers (Josh 9:23, 27).

Forgiveness

Israel's subsequent military victories imply that they had been forgiven by God (Jos 10–11). In fact, the book of Joshua ends on a relatively high note: the Israelites had taken control of significant

16. Later, they will be given to the tribe of Benjamin (Josh 18:25–28). For the connection between the Gibeonites and the serpent, cf. *Gen. Rab.* 20.5.

portions of Canaan, and they renewed their commitment to serve the LORD and finish the conquest (Josh 24).

In addition to these to landmark sins found in the book of Joshua, the book of Judges recounts the ever-deepening, downward spiral of sin and self-destruction that the tribes of Israel experienced: they were *not vigilant* in following the LORD and continuing the conquest of the land, they were *deceived* into doing what is evil in the sight of the LORD, they became *aware of their sin* and cried out to the LORD for deliverance, and they were *forgiven* and delivered from their rebellion through a judge.[17]

4. Division (Judg)

Division

The book of Judges relates the growing division between Judah and the rest of the tribes of Israel by consistently portraying Judah positively and non-Judah tribes—especially Ephraim, Levi, and Benjamin—negatively.[18] With regard to Judah, the book is framed with Judah portrayed as Israel's leader in being the first to obey God's command to conquer the land and to deliver God's judgment on wicked Benjamin (Judg 1:1–2; 20:18), and the opening survey of the twelve tribes' conquest of their allotted lands devotes significantly more space to Judah and portrays them as the most

17. In fact, the book of Judges can be seen as comprising several mini-cycles of peace, apostasy, oppression, and deliverance, which is similar to the basic cycle proposed throughout this work.

18. In addition, other factors show a division between Judah and the other Israelite tribes. For example, Deborah and Barak's song in Judg 5 implies a division between the northern and southern tribes: they suppose that Ephraim, Benjamin, Manasseh, Zebulun, Issachar, Reuben, Dan, Asher, and Naphtali should respond to their battle call, while Judah is not even mentioned (Manasseh is included in Machir and Gilead [Num 32:39–40; 36:1; Deut 3:13; Josh 13:29–31]; Levi is not mentioned since it was a priestly tribe and not supposed to fight; Simeon is not mentioned either, but its ambiguous location in the south may have connected it with Judah more than with the other tribes). For other examples of this division, cf. 1 Sam 11:8; 15:4.

successful in their task (Judg 1:1–20).[19] Additionally, Othniel—Judah's only judge—is portrayed as the ideal judge: he was the first judge mentioned, he obeyed God fully, and he was the only judge able to unite all Israel under his judgeship (Judg 3:7–11).[20]

With regard to non-Judah tribes, all of them are chastised in various ways throughout the book, but Ephraim, Levi, and Benjamin receive especially harsh condemnation. Ephraim is the tribe mentioned most throughout the book of Judges,[21] and although they insist that they be regarded as the leaders of the (northern) tribes (Judg 7:24–8:3; 12:1), their involvement never leads Israel out of its spiritual darkness. Instead, in Judges 17, the author lampoons an Ephraimite named Micah by showing him to break virtually every established decree about the right worship of God (cf. Deut 12; 18:1–5[22]): he sets up a cultic site, makes an idol, consecrates his own (underage) priest, pays the priest with silver and clothes, and does what is right in his own eyes. Levi only shows up at the end of the book (Judg 17–21), and is portrayed as apostate: the tribe essentially breaks all of the rules established in Deuteronomy 12–13 for the right worship of the Lord.[23] As for

19. Additionally, the fact that Jael, a Kenite from Judah, was able to kill Sisera and thus defeat Jabin and the Canaanites—something which even Barak was unable to do (Judg 4:9)—may suggest that the author of Judges was trying to insinuate either that Judah's wisdom was superior to that of the other tribes, or that the least of Judah were better than the best of non-Judah.

20. With all the other judges, individual tribes are said to have rallied (or not) around them (except Samuel, who did not rally any tribe). With Othniel, no particular tribes are mentioned, only "Israel." Granted this is an argument from silence, but it appears to be an intentional silence on the part of the biblical author.

21. Judges 1:29; 2:9; 3:27; 4:5; 5:14; 10:1, 9; 12:1–6, 15; 17:1, 8; 18:2, 13; 19:1, 16, 18.

22. O'Connell, *Rhetoric of the Book of Judges*, 239–40. Going one step further, Judg 17–18 violates much of Deut 12, and Judg 19–21 violates much of Deut 13 (O'Connell, *Rhetoric of the Book of Judges*, 230–31). Judges 18:1–10 evokes Israel's sending out of the twelve spies in Num 12:16–14:45, and Judg 19:14–28 evokes the description of Sodom's sin in Gen 19:1–11 (O'Connell, *Rhetoric of the Book of Judges*, 265). In other words, Judg ends with some of the worst rebellion and judgment stories of the Pentateuch.

23. O'Connell, *Rhetoric of the Book of Judges*, 230–31, 239–40, 256–57.

Benjamin, the book of Judges portrays them as Judah's foil: they could not conquer Jebus (i.e., Jerusalem), whereas Judah did (Judg 1:8, 21), and when Benjamin apostatizes, it is Judah who is first in line to carry out God's judgment on them (Judg 20:18).[24]

All of this has the cumulative effect of pitting righteous Judah against the unrighteous non-Judah tribes, especially Ephraim, Levi, and Benjamin. This will become important as the story progresses, since the next three major figures in the biblical story will come from these three tribes: Samuel will be an Ephraimite, Eli a Levite, and Saul a Benjaminite. In short, the book of Judges is preparing its readers for God's judgment on Eli and Saul and the resolution of the Ephraim–Judah rivalry through Samuel's (Ephraim) anointing of David (Judah).[25]

Persecution

To say nothing of the persecution that the Israelites received at the hands of their numerous invaders, the book of Judges shows how Israel became its own persecutor as the various tribes turn on each other,[26] with some of their own judges taking the lead at times (e.g., Abimelech).[27] Although they were supposed to shepherd

24. Additionally, the Benjaminite Ehud is Israel's second judge (Judg 3:12–30), and his left-handedness may be a gesture toward Benjamin's deviancy, which will manifest itself at the end of the book and in Saul's reign. Ironically, aside from the Othniel story, it is only in the final chapters of Judges—where Israel is depicted at its worst—that Israel is united and Levites are mentioned. In chapter 19, Benjamin is depicted as Sodom and Gomorrah, and in chapter 20, the sack of the Benjaminite town Gibeah is depicted as the sack of Ai.

25. "[T]he rhetorical purpose of the book of Judges is ostensibly to enjoin its readers to endorse a divinely appointed Judahite king who, in contrast to foreign kings or non-Judahite deliverers in Israel, upholds such deuteronomic ideals as the need to expel foreigners from the land and the need to maintain intertribal loyalty to YHWH's cult and his regulations concerning social justice" (O'Connell, *Rhetoric of the Book of Judges*, 343; cf. 266, 272).

26. Judges 8:1–3; 12:1–6; 20:1–48; 21:10–11.

27. "Abimelech turns the sanctuary where Joshua renewed God's covenant with Israel (Josh 8:30–35; 24:1–28) into a war zone, killing off the inhabitants of Shechem and finally falling prey himself to an unexpected murderer. Ephraim constantly picks fights with judges from other tribes (8:1; 12:1),

God's people (1 Chr 11:2),[28] they ended up scattering and killing them for their own profit (cf. Jer 23:1–2; Ezek 34:1–6). While the central portion of Judges (chapters 3–16) relates Israel's persecution, the opening and concluding portions (chapters 1–2; 17–21) relate that the reason why: they were persecuted because of their idolatry and moral wickedness.

Cities

God commanded the Israelites to take over Canaan and its cities, which at least occasionally involved renaming them (e.g., Judg 1:10–11). Instead, they often failed in this task, and thus the old city names remained (Judg 19:10). When they did name new cities, they often reflected national tragedies (Judg 2:1–5), and Benjamin even rebuilt cities that were under the ban (Judg 20:48; 21:23).

Apostasy; inter-marriage

Israel's failure to possess the land because of their spiritual apostasy is the central theme of the book of Judges (Judg 1:1–3:6). It hardly took a generation to pass after the death of Joshua for Israel to forsake God and serve the Baals and Ashtaroths of Canaan (Judg 2:1–13). As Judges 3:1–6 illustrates, Israel's intermarriage with the Canaanites invariably brought about apostasy (cf. Judg 3:7; 10:6).[29] Whereas Israel had been called to "Israelitize" Canaan, some have argued that the purpose of the book of Judges is to demonstrate the "Canaanization" of Israel, a view which, even if a bit overstated, nevertheless captures a central theme of

---

resulting finally in a civil war in which Gilead destroys 42,000 Ephraimites (12:6). This theme of violence reappears in chaps. 17–21 when a lurid story of false worship, rape, and the splitting of a woman's body into twelve pieces erupts into a confrontation between all Israel and Benjamin, whereby the tribe of Benjamin is almost eliminated from existence" (Butler, *Judges*, lx).

28. Second Sam 7:7 may also refer to the judges as "shepherds," but this involves textual emendation, as the MT and LXX both read "tribes."

29. Marvin Sweeney refers to the intermarriage with pagan nations mentioned in Judg 3:1–6 as the "basic problem" of the book ("Davidic Polemics," 529).

the book.[30] Instead of overcoming the chaotic forces of evil in the name of the LORD as they had been commanded to do (Deut 7:1–5), they allowed themselves to be defeated through intermarriage and its inevitable apostasy.[31]

The turning point in the book of Judges comes in chapter 10, after Gideon had set up an idolatrous ephod (Judg 8:24–27) and Abimelek had become a murderer of his own people (Judg 9).[32] In chapter 10, although Israel cries out for deliverance, God responds by advising them to call out to the gods that they had chosen over him (Judg 10:10–16). By the end of the book, the Israelites had become worse than their Canaanite neighbors: the most basic of social expectations were no longer present (e.g., Judg 19:15),[33] and some of Israel's most important tribes had been completely corrupted: the Levites (Israel's supposed spiritual leaders), Ephraimites (Israel's supposed civil leaders), Danites (who will be wiped from Israel's inheritance), and Benjaminites (from whom Saul will come). Judges 18:1–10 evokes Israel's sending out of the twelve spies in Numbers 12:16–14:45, and Judges 19:14–28 evokes the description of Sodom's sin in Genesis 19:1–11.[34] In other words, the book of Judges ends with some of the worst rebellion and judgment stories of the Pentateuch. At this point, each man was doing what was right in his own eyes (Judg 17:6; 21:25),[35] thereby recalling the antediluvian situation in which the thoughts of men were

30. The term "Canaanization" apparently originated with Daniel Block, who claims that "several" interpreters have followed him (*Judges*, 58). He states that the underlying cause of this "Canaanization" is "the tribes's failure to fulfill the divine mandate in eliminating the native population" (*Judges*, 58).

31. This is reminiscent of David's decision to stay in Jerusalem in the spring when kings were supposed to go to war (2 Sam 11:1).

32. These two sins can be seen as representative of all sins found in Scripture: idolatry is the worst sin against God and murder is the worst sin against man. After Judg 8:28, the land of Israel will no longer be said to enjoy rest.

33. As one author has put it, 'The book of Judges clearly and consciously reverses all that Joshua accomplished' (Butler, *Judges*, lvii). The evil of God's people being worse than the evil of others is mentioned elsewhere in Scripture (e.g., Ezek 23:11).

34. O'Connell, *Rhetoric of the Book of Judges*, 265.

35. Moses had warned them not to do this in Deut 12:8.

only evil continually (Gen 6:5, 11–12). The Israelites failed to drive out the Canaanites, and thus they continued to live in the land for hundreds of years to come (1 Kgs 9:20–21).

Noticeably absent during this period is any mention of the tabernacle and ark: aside from some parenthetical comments,[36] they are never discussed or treated in any length, the LORD is never consulted there, and when the ark does enter the story, Israel tries to use it as a magical totem to save them in battle (1 Sam 4:1–11).

Prophet; preacher of righteousness

The book of Judges names twelve judges, but six of them—sometimes ministering in pairs—receive extensive treatment: Othniel, Ehud, Deborah/Barak, Gideon/Abimelech, Jephthah, and Samson. They were supposed to function similarly to prophets or preachers of righteousness and call the people back to the LORD (cf. Judg 6:7–10), but often this did not happen: all but Othniel had their moral failure, and the last three were more wicked than good.[37] It is significant to note that these three wicked judges were oppressively violent and sexually promiscuous, again evoking key themes found in the antediluvian period.[38] On occasion, God would send prophets to call Israel back to himself, but their cries only had limited effect (Judg 6:7–10; cf. 10:10–16).

36. Joshua 18:1; Judg 18:31; 20:27; 21:12, 19, 21; 1 Sam 2:22; 3:3. Aside from the story of the ark's capture in 1 Sam 4:1–7:2, the ark will not come back into prominence until 2 Sam 6, when David brings it to Jerusalem. In fact, from 1 Sam 7 to 2 Sam 6, aside from one textually debatable case in 1 Sam 14:18 where "ephod" appears to be the preferred reading, the ark is not mentioned at all.

37. With the exception of Samuel, this pattern continues into 1 Sam; cf. 1 Sam 4:18 (Eli) and 8:1–3 (Samuel's sons).

38. Ironically, however, God's Spirit did come down on Gideon (Judg 6:34), Jephthah (Judg 11:29), and Samson (Judg 13:25; 14:6, 19; 15:14), something which did not happen even to good judges such as Ehud and Deborah. This should be interpreted more as extolling God's mercy than as approving the Israelites's conduct.

Boaz came seven generations after Judah (Ruth 4:12, 18–21), and therefore ten generations after Abraham.[39] He is introduced as a mighty/worthy man, and later is referred to as a redeemer (Ruth 2:1; 3:9, 12). Although not technically a prophet or preacher of righteousness, his actions throughout the book, combined with the piety he modeled and inspired in others (Ruth 2:4), call to mind someone like Enoch, who walked with God.

Affliction; 'crying out'

The Israelites repeatedly found themselves in great distress and cried out to the LORD for salvation (e.g., Judg 2:15, 18). Although he would answer, the deliverance was only temporary: when God's appointed judge died, the people returned to their apostasy (e.g., Judg 2:19). The people continually 'cried out' to God because of their oppression (e.g., Judg 3:9; 4:3; 10:12; 2 Sam 7:10), but rarely if ever did they cry out in repentance.[40]

5. Judgment (1 Sam 1–4)

Chaos; flood

The book of Judges ends with the refrain that summarizes the entire period of the judges, but which had become increasingly more serious as the period drew to a close: "Everyone did what was right in his own eyes" (Judg 21:25; cf. 17:6).[41] By the opening of 1 Samuel, the priesthood had become severely compromised (1 Sam 2:12–17, 22–25), the word of the LORD was rare (1 Sam 3:1), and God had chosen to reveal himself not to a Levitical priest or prophet, but to an Ephraimite boy: Samuel (1 Sam 3:1–4:1). Eli's lack of insight and vision (1 Sam 1:12–13; 3:2; 4:15) combined

39. Boaz can also be seen as the seventh generation from Perez, which may explain the benediction found in Ruth 4:12 (Sasson, "A Genealogical 'Convention,'" 184).

40. Butler, *Judges*, lxxviii.

41. The author also provides the reason this was so: Israel had no king (Judg 17:6; 18:1; 19:1; 21:25). This will be remedied in the monarchy, especially under David.

with his greed and obesity (1 Sam 2:29, 32; 4:18) remind one of Isaac's conditions—physical and spiritual—in his old age, after he had stopped being vigilant and failed to trust in the LORD. In short, chaos reigned amongst the Israelites.

Exile; expulsion

Since Samson had not completed the task of saving the Israelites from the Philistines, at the time of Eli and Samuel, the Philistines were still their overlords, thus making the Israelites captives in their own land. What is worse, the ark of the covenant was captured (1 Sam 4), and the Scriptural language and imagery evoke many themes associated with exile: the Philistines cleanly routed the Israelites and subjugated them, which the text calls a 'plague,'[42] Eli and his sons were rejected by God and killed (1 Sam 4:11, 18),[43] and the ark of the LORD was carried away captive and placed in Dagon's temple as a sign of defeat (1 Sam 4:11; 5:1–2).[44] Instead of using God's ark as a place to seek his will and guidance, Israel had used it as a magical totem, thinking they could force God to do their sinful will (1 Sam 4:3–4). It is no wonder that Phineas's wife named her son Ichabod, since God's glory had departed from Israel (1 Sam 4:19–22). God had rejected Shiloh, the place where the tabernacle dwelt.[45] It is significant to note

42. First Sam 4:2, 9, 17 (cf. Exod 9:15; 1 Sam 6:4).

43. God's judgment on Eli's household is prolonged, yet absolute: first the destruction of his household is prophesied (1 Sam 2:27–36); then it comes to initial fulfillment when the Philistines kill his two sons, Hophni and Phinehas (1 Sam 4:11); then it is further fulfilled when Saul kills the priests at Nob (1 Sam 22:11–23; cf. 1 Sam 14:3, 18); finally it comes to complete fulfillment when Solomon expels Abiathar from the priesthood (1 Kgs 2:26–27).

44. The fact that the ark was captive for seven months means that the Israelites were left without recourse to purge their sins, which was a major problem (1 Sam 6:1). As the ark was returned during the wheat harvest (1 Sam 6:14), which normally occurred in May–June, this means that the ark was absent during the festival of Passover and perhaps Pentecost, but not Tabernacles or the Day of Atonement.

45. Jeremiah 7:12–14; 26:4–9; Ps 78:59–64. It is possible that the MT reading of 1 Sam 2:29a, 32a identifies the Elides as the "enemy" of the temple at

that the ark will not come back into prominence until 2 Samuel 6, when David brings it to Jerusalem.

Deliverance of righteous remnant

Nevertheless, God preserved a righteous remnant. This has already been seen with the tribe of Judah: their brief appearances in the book of Judges are consistently positive, and they do not appear to partake in the widespread apostasy present in the other tribes of Israel. At a specific level, a righteous remnant can also be seen in the story of Boaz (from Judah) and his wife Ruth, who will become the great-grandparents of king David, whose ancestors maintained their faith during this time (Ruth 4:17–22). Additionally, Elkanah (from Ephraim) and his wives Hannah and Peninnah also did not succumb to evil in their day, and from Hannah came Samuel (1 Sam 1:1–3, 19–20).

Samuel (from Ephraim) will anoint two men as kings of Israel. The first one, Saul (from Benjamin), is the people's choice, and will fall away from God and be rejected by him. The second one, David (from Judah), is God's choice, and will be a man after God's own heart. This double anointing resolves the Joseph–Judah rivalry that began during the patriarchal cycle, as well as the possible claim that Benjamin could make for being Jacob's beloved son and Rachel's only son who didn't marry a foreigner (as Joseph had done in Egypt). Thus, the potential ambiguity and rivalry is settled as Ephraim (Samuel) recognizes Judah (David) as Israel's true king. From here on, it will be certain that God's representative minority through whom he will bless the rest of the world will not run through Ephraim (or Benjamin), but rather through Judah, although the majority of Judahites will themselves prove faithless as well.

Shiloh; cf. Kim, "Eli, 'Enemy of a Temple'?"

Chapter 6: David, Representing One Tribe of Israel

2 Samuel–2 Kings

APPROXIMATELY 400 YEARS AFTER the Exodus and Conquest, God recreated again through David. By Jacob's prophecy (Gen 49:8–12), Judah had been chosen to lead Israel, and through their example during the period of the judges, they had proven themselves able to do so. The book of Ruth focuses on the line of Boaz and Ruth, from whom David will come. Of the many Israelites in his day, only David was identified as following God's own heart (1 Sam 13:14; cf. Acts 13:22). From now on, the king will represent Israel, and the latter's destiny will be bound up with the former's. Several stages in this cycle are quite protracted: the beginning of the cycle recounts the exodus of the ark and the rise of David, the middle of the cycle is extended during the reigns of David and Solomon—the first as the preparer and the latter as the fulfiller—, and the end of the cycle recounts the division and judgment of the northern and southern kingdoms. This cycle includes the largest number of biblical books, including many of the writing prophets.

Cullmann's principle of representation comes strongly into view here. Although Israel's geographic expansion will reach its height under the reigns of David and Solomon,[1] it will be short

1. First Kgs 4:21 [MT: 5:1]; but cf. 9:16.

lived, and after the split between the northern and southern kingdoms, the geographic focus will be centered on the southern kingdom, roughly overlapping with the tribal allotment of Judah.[2]

1. Creation (1 Sam 5–2 Sam 5)

Creation from chaos

The background to the rise of David was a rejected priesthood and king—Eli and Saul, respectively—which had led to a subjugated people (1 Sam 8:10–18). Although Saul's reign began promisingly (1 Sam 11; cf. 14:47–48), he soon stopped following God, and thus was rejected by him (1 Sam 13:8–14; cf. 15:10–11, 27–29). The rest of his life was marked by sin and death: he became obsessed with killing David (1 Sam 18:10–1, etc.), murdered innocent priests (1 Sam 22:6–19), visited necromancers (1 Sam 28), and met a shameful death in battle (1 Sam 31:1–4). By Saul's end, the Philistines had routed the Israelites in battle and taken over their lands (1 Sam 31:7). What is more, Saul's son, Ish-bosheth, had been anointed king over the northern tribes of Israel (2 Sam 2:8–9).[3] Thus, what little unity remained in Israel was centered on one of Saul's descendants, who most likely shared his father's tyrannical spirit. Israel finds itself leaderless, dispossessed of its land, impoverished, and spiritually malnourished.

Creation battle

As 1 Samuel 4 recounts a type of exile for Israel as it loses the ark of the covenant in a lost battle to the Philistines, 1 Samuel 5 begins to recount a type of new creation, especially as it centers on the destiny of the ark of the Lord. The ark's experiences are filtered

2. The author of Kgs relates the shrinking size of Israel and Judah at several points throughout the narrative (2 Kgs 3; 8:20–22; 10:32–33).

3. Saul's physical dominance and attractiveness make him the perfect foil for the poor, young, short, red-haired David (1 Sam 16:7, 11–12; 17:42; 18:23), although David does have many good qualities as well (1 Sam 16:18).

through various Exodus motifs.[4] As the Israelites had 'come out' of bondage from Egypt (Exod 13:3, 14; 20:2), now the ark comes out of bondage from the house of Dagan (1 Sam 5:1–2). As the Egyptians had been stricken with plagues and death (Exod 7–11; cf. 3:20), now the Philistines are struck with tumors and death (1 Sam 5:6, 9–12). As the Egyptians had sought to rid themselves of the Israelites lest they die (Exod 10:7; 11:8; 12:30–33), now the Philistines seek to rid themselves of the ark lest they die (1 Sam 5:11; 6:2). As God had struck the Egyptians with his hand (e.g., Exod 3:19–20), now the hand of the LORD is heavy on the Philistines (1 Sam 5:6–7, 9; 6:3, 5). As flies had 'destroyed' the land of Egypt (Exod 8:24), now mice 'destroy' the land of Philistia (1 Sam 6:5).[5] As Pharaoh had consulted with his wise men and magicians (Exod 7:11), now the Philistine lords consult with their priests and diviners (1 Sam 6:2). As the LORD had executed judgment on the gods of Egypt (Exod 12:12), now the ark executes judgment on Dagon (1 Sam 5:1–4; 6:5). As the Egyptians had 'cried out' when their firstborn sons were slain (Exod 11:6; 12:30), now the inhabitants of Ekron 'cry out' in their distress (1 Sam 5:10). As the Israelites had left Egypt with gifts (Exod 3:21–22; 11:2–3; 12:35–36), now the ark returns to Israel with gifts (1 Sam 6:2–5). The Philistines even admonished themselves not to harden their hearts as Pharaoh and the Egyptians had done (1 Sam 6:6).[6]

4. For many of these observations, cf. Campbell, *The Ark*, 199–205; Daube, *The Exodus Pattern*, 73–88.

5. This same verb is used in Gen 6:17 to refer to God's 'destruction' of all flesh.

6. As Antony Campbell concludes his study of the parallels between the two stories, "There is more than enough material here to justify the comparison with the Exodus. If the comparison is accepted, the narrative, after laying bare the end of that history which began with the first Exodus, proceeds to depict the sovereign movement of Yahweh as a second Exodus" (*Ark Narrative*, 204). He also suggests another parallel, namely, that as the Israelites wandered in the wilderness, the ark wandered throughout the Philistine land (*Ark Narrative*, 204 n. 3). For these and other connections, cf. Daube, *Exodus Pattern*, 73–88. Another parallel may be the duration of the plagues: the first plague in Egypt lasted seven days (Exod 7:25) and the plague in Philistia lasted seven months (1 Sam 6:1); cf. Klein, *1 Samuel*, 56.

After Saul's death and David's anointing as king of Judah, David defeats Ish-bosheth (2 Sam 2:12–32), conquers Jebus (2 Sam 5:6–10), defeats the Philistines (2 Sam 5:17–25), and subdues Israel's neighbors (2 Sam 8:1–14; 10). In short, Israel's internal and external foes are eliminated as a threat to Israel.

God's Spirit

God takes his Spirit away from Saul and gives it to David (1 Sam 16:13–14), and he knows that God's holy Spirit is with him (Ps 51:11). His numerous musical compositions demonstrate his lifelong communion with the Spirit, even explicitly claiming that some of his lyrics come from the Spirit himself (2 Sam 23:2).

God's word

With the establishment of the temple in Jerusalem and the placement of the ark in the Most Holy Place, the Ten Words that God had given to Moses at Mount Sinai have arrived in Jerusalem (1 Kgs 8:9). The societal order that God had established through the reigns of David and Solomon were completed and perfected by the moral order represented in the Ten Words.

Temple

One of David's first acts after defeating the Philistines was to bring the ark of the Lord to Jerusalem and offer sacrifices before him (2 Sam 6:17).[7] This was a very important moment in biblical history since it was the first time since mankind's banishment from the garden of Eden that God's people had controlled this mountain

7. David brought the ark into a tent that he had prepared for it. It is uncertain if this is the same as the tent of meeting used from the time of Moses onward (1 Kgs 8:4; 2 Chr 1:3).

and established a cultic site there.[8] Later, the LORD will instruct David to build an altar to the LORD (2 Sam 24:18–25).[9]

With the arrival of Solomon to the throne, the original plan from the time of the Exodus has been fulfilled: God has chosen his mountain and established his temple where his people can worship him (Deut 12:5–14).[10] As with creation and the tabernacle before, the temple is built from plunder taken from Israel's enemies (1 Chr 26:27). As the glory of the LORD, manifested as a cloud, had filled the tabernacle that Moses had made, now again his glory fills the temple that David and Solomon had made (1 Kgs 8:10–11).[11] King Solomon decorated the temple with flowers (lilies), fruits (pomegranates), and trees (palm trees), probably to resemble the garden of Eden. Also it is possible that living trees (esp. olive) were growing in the temple courts, which would be an even stronger link with the garden.[12] Whereas Babel had been

8. Jerusalem had been inhabited by Canaanites after the flood (Gen 10:15–19) and during the times of Abraham (e.g., Gen 12:6), the Conquest (Josh 15:63), and the judges (Judg 1:21). The only known exception to their occupation may have been Melchizedek, whose role at Jebus is uncertain (Gen 14:18–20).

9. Although David wanted to build a house for the LORD, it was the LORD who promised to build a house for David: it would not be a physical house, but rather a lineage (2 Sam 7:2, 11). As the LORD had blessed the tabernacle with his sanctifying presence, he promised to be with David's descendants (2 Sam 7:14–16). David was permitted to plan and prepare for the temple (1 Chr 28–29), which would be carried out by his son, Solomon (1 Kgs 5:1–6:38; 7:13–8:11; 2 Chr 2:1–5:1). In response to God's gracious hand upon him, David wrote Ps 18 in which he evokes various themes from creation and the Exodus (cf. 2 Sam 22).

10. Moses' earlier prophecy of "the place, O LORD, which you have made for your abode" (Exod 15:17) is fulfilled in Solomon's temple (1 Kgs 8:13; cf. 2 Chr 6:2).

11. Solomon built the temple that his father had planned (1 Kgs 5:1–6:38; 7:13–8:11; 2 Chr 2:1–5:1).

12. Genesis 2:9; 1 Kgs 6:18, 29; 7:18–26, 49; Ps 52:8; 92:12. Marvin Tate writes: "There is little reason to doubt (as some do) that olive trees actually grew in the area of the temple on Mount Zion. Cypress and olive trees grow in the Dome of the Rock area of Jerusalem today. Trees were common in temple areas throughout the ancient Near East, symbols of life, fertility, and power" (*Psalms 51–100*, 38). Othmar Keel similarly argues that the temple trees were

built for the name of its builders, the Jerusalem temple was built for the name of the LORD (1 Kgs 8:20). In this sense, Mount Zion functions as a kind of anti-Tower of Babel.

Rest

The opening chapters of 2 Samuel relate how God firmly established David in his kingdom and gave him 'rest' from all his enemies (2 Sam 5:12; 7:1). Similarly, he also gave 'rest' to Solomon and the whole of Israel (1 Kgs 5:4; 8:56). Although David had been a man of bloodshed, Solomon was a son of 'rest' (1 Chr 22:6–10, 17–19; cf. 28:3). Indeed, Solomon's initial reign was a time of peace (1 Kgs 4:26 [MT: 5:4]).

2. Man (2 Sam 5–10)

Election

Whereas previously all Israel had been called God's son (e.g., Exod 4:22), now there is a sense in which the king is God's unique son (e.g., Ps 2:7). David's election began in 1 Samuel 16:6–13 when he was anointed the true king of Israel, but for the next several years he will remain a servant of king Saul and be persecuted by him. Thus, in another sense, David's election did not begin until after the death of Saul, especially in 2 Samuel 5–7.[13]

As Israel—the smallest and least significant among the nations—had been chosen by God to be his people (Deut 7:7–8), so too was David—the youngest amongst his impressive cast of brothers—chosen by God to be king of Israel (1 Sam 16:6–13). Before being king, David had been a shepherd (1 Sam 16:11), which will become the dominant imagery for the kings's relationship to

---

living reminders of God's invisible, mysterious blessing which was operative in them and in his people (*Symbolism*, 135–36, 354).

13. As Antony Campbell writes, "If 1 Sam 4 marks the end of an epoch, 2 Sam 6 marks a new beginning, the resumption of Yahweh's relationship with Israel. In this sense, it also marks the legitimation of the new thing that has been begun in Jerusalem. Salvation history can be said to be resumed" (*Ark Narrative*, 201).

Israel.[14] David is the fourteenth generation from Abraham, which again, surely cannot be mere coincidence.[15] As with previously chosen men, David is portrayed as a prophet (2 Sam 23:2; cf. Acts 2:30), priest (e.g., 2 Sam 6:17–18; 24:25), and king (2 Sam 5:1–5). Similarly, Solomon will be portrayed as a prophet (1 Kgs 3:5; 6:11; 9:2;[16] cf. *Ps. Sol.* 2:24–35), priest (1 Kgs 3:3–4; 8:5, 14, 64), and king (e.g., 1 Kgs 1:34).

Formed outside; 'go forth'

David is from the small town of Bethlehem which, although in the region of Judah, was not a particularly important city (1 Sam 16:1; Mic 5:2). Since the future ruler of Israel will be said to 'go forth' from Bethlehem (Mic 5:2), a similar 'going forth' could arguably be attributed to David as well. During his time of persecution under Saul, David was forced to live in the wilderness (e.g., 1 Sam 23:14–15). Near the end of Saul's reign, the pressure became so intense that he exiled himself to Philistia (1 Sam 27:1–7). However, shortly after Saul's death, David went up to Hebron (2 Sam 2:1–4).[17]

Mixed multitude

David took many wives and concubines, before and after becoming king, which resulted in him having many children with different mothers (2 Sam 2:2; 5:13; cf. 15:16). David's love for women will prove to be his downfall, and his children will fight with each over the kingdom.

14. Second Sam 5:2; 1 Chr 11:2; 21:17; Ps 78:70–72; Jer 2:8; 3:15; 23:1–4; Ezek 34:1–6. Mesha, king of Moab, was involved in breeding sheep (2 Kgs 3:4), but there does not appear to be any significant connection between his occupation and his fitness to care for his people.

15. First Chr 1:27–28, 34; 2:1, 4–5, 9–12, 15; Ruth 4:12, 18–22.

16. The language of the Lord "appearing" (Heb: ראה, *ra'ah*) to someone is used in Gen 12:7 with reference to Abraham, who was, indeed, called a prophet (Gen 20:7).

17. God promised David that descendants would 'go forth' from David to rule after him (2 Sam 7:12).

Mountain and garden

David conquered Jerusalem (Jebus), the highest mountain in the area,[18] and brought the ark of the LORD to one of its high points (2 Sam 5:6–10; 24:18–25).[19] It is likely that David's residence resembled a garden-like atmosphere: garden-like palaces were common for rulers in antiquity (e.g., Esth 1:5; 7:1), and gardens are known to have been in Jerusalem throughout the divided monarchy period and beyond,[20] which makes their presence during the time of David a reasonable supposition.[21]

Solomon was acclaimed king at Gihon, a river at Jerusalem that carries the same name as one of the four rivers in Eden (1 Kgs 1:33, 38, 45). Just before dying, David charged him to 'keep' God's laws, thus evoking Adam's call to 'keep' the garden and the priestly duty to 'keep' the tabernacle/temple (1 Kgs 2:2–3). He had mastery knowledge of flora and fauna (1 Kgs 4:33 [MT: 5:13]), and his triennial shipments included animals that would inhabit a royal garden (1 Kgs 10:22), all of which evoke the idea of Solomon in a garden-like atmosphere.

Solomon will build the temple at an even higher point on the mountain than where his father had set up the ark of the

18. Mount Hermon to the north is higher. Interestingly, according to Isa 2:1–2, in the eschaton God will raise Jerusalem to be even higher (Mic 4:1; Zech 14:10).

19. The texts that evoke the mountain feature are numerous: Ps 2:6; 3:4; 15:1; 24:3; 43:3; 48:1–2; 74:2; 78:54; 87:1–3; Isa 30:29; 56:7; 57:13; 65:25; 66:20. According to Justin Martyr, Jews of his day were conceptualizing salvation as having an inheritance on the "holy mountain of God" (*Dialogue*, 25).

20. First Kgs 21:1; 2 Kgs 21:18, 26; 25:4; Jer 52:7; Neh 3:15. First Kgs 10:22 implies the presence of a zoo of some kind, which in turn may imply a garden where they lived. If Solomon is the author of Eccl, it would place gardens in Jerusalem immediately after David (Eccl 2:4–8).

21. Another interesting garden parallel may be present here. Genesis 2:12 says that the river Pishon flowed around Havilah—which many identify with Arabia—where there was much gold, and in 1 Kgs 10, the Queen of Sheba—which many identify with Arabia—gave Solomon 120 talents of gold, making his treasures so vast that silver was considered worthless (1 Kgs 10:10–11, 21). Thus, the gold mentioned in Gen 2:12 has finally been brought to Eden by the Queen of Sheba in her gift to Solomon.

covenant,[22] thereby simultaneously evoking and heightening the man–mountain–garden constellation (1 Kgs 8:1–4; 2 Chr 3:1).[23]

Divine blessing and commands

David was blessed by God and promised descendants (2 Sam 7:1, 4–17, 29; Ps 132:11–12). His household multiplied greatly (2 Sam 5:13–16), and he 'subdued' and ruled over the surrounding nations.[24] All this implies that the original creational commands had been handed on to, and at least partially fulfilled by, David.[25] In short, God had made a covenant with David (cf. Ps 89:1–37), which is known as the Davidic covenant. The blessing of the Abrahamic covenant now passes on to the king of Israel (Ps 72:17).

God also blessed Solomon: under him, the people became so great that they could not be numbered, thus evoking both the original creation mandate and the promise given to Abraham (1 Kgs 3:8). He 'had dominion' from the Euphrates to Egypt (1 Kgs 4:24 [MT: 5:1]).[26] Solomon was 'blessed' by God and the people (1 Kgs 2:45; 8:66). Similar to how Joshua had claimed that "not one word had failed" of all the promises that God had made to the patriarchs (Josh 23:14), Solomon claimed that "not one word has failed" of all the promises that God had made through Moses (1 Kgs 8:55–56).[27] As the serpent and its cursed seed were to lick

22. Several texts (e.g., 2 Sam 24:18–20; 2 Chr 5:5) demonstrate that the City of David, that is, Zion (cf. 2 Sam 5:7), was lower than where the temple was built.

23. According to Ezekiel, the eschatological temple will also be on a mountain, with lush vegetation, and with rivers flowing forth from it (Ezek 47:1, 12). Adding to the garden theme, some texts refer to the Israelite people with garden imagery, especially in connection with their presence in the temple (2 Sam 7:10; Ps 52:8; 80:8–11; 92:12–14).

24. Second Sam 8–10 [esp. 8:11]; cf. Ps 2:8; 72:8; 110:2.

25. Also important to note is Ps 72:17, where David (or Solomon) states that all the nations will be blessed in the king of Israel, thereby evoking part of the original Abrahamic covenant (Gen 12:3).

26. Also to be noticed is the reference to the Euphrates, making yet another connection with the creation account (Gen 2:14).

27. The Hebrew expression is the same in both texts.

the dust (Gen 3:14), so too were the king's enemies to lick the dust (Ps 72:9).

3. Fall[28] (2 Sam 11; 1 Kgs 11)

Not vigilant

Instead of being vigilant and expanding God's kingdom as he had done in the past, at some point in David's reign he stayed behind in Jerusalem and did not go out to battle (2 Sam 11:1). Perhaps it was a passivity that was hardly noticeable: after all, he had just subdued all his internal and external threats, and his army commander, Joab, was currently winning battles abroad (2 Sam 11:1). Whatever the cause may have been, the decision to abdicate his kingly responsibility and stay behind in Jerusalem was the beginning of his downfall.

A similar lack of vigilance was present during Solomon's reign. While it is true that the beginning of Solomon's downfall is summarized in 1 Kings 11, on several prior occasions the author records that Solomon had taken an Egyptian wife (1 Kgs 3:1; 7:8; 9:16, 24). This repeated connection between Solomon and Egypt is not arbitrary, as the author is implying that Solomon was slowly taking the country back to Egyptian slavery: the hard service and heavy yoke he placed on his people evokes the Egyptians' treatment of the Israelites during their slavery (1 Kgs 12:4; cf. Exod 1:14; 6:9; Lev 26:13), his use of forced labor evokes the tower of Babel and Egypt (1 Kgs 4:6; 11:28; 12:18), and his building of store cities evokes the Egyptian store cities Pithom and Rameses (1 Kgs 9:19; cf. Exod 1:11). Despite what is written about the expected conduct of an Israelite king in Deuteronomy 17:14–17, Solomon let a foreigner rule over his subjects (1 Kgs 9:11), acquired horses for himself (1 Kgs 10:26–29), greatly multiplied his wives (1 Kgs 11:3), and amassed excessive amounts silver and gold for himself (1 Kgs 10:14–15, 27). Although he had prayed to discern between good and evil (1 Kgs 3:9), he failed like Adam and Eve before him.

28. For many of these parallels, cf. Gage, *Gospel of Genesis*, 68–69.

Woman; deception/seduction; usurpation

Similar to the sin of Achan, David's sin is described in terms that have numerous linguistic parallels with Eve's sin in Genesis 3:6: David 'saw' Bathsheba, noticed that she was 'good' and very beautiful, inquired after her (thereby evoking Eve's dialogue with the serpent), and 'took' her (2 Sam 11:2–4). As Adam and Eve had known good and evil, so too did David 'know' Bathsheba (cf. Gen 4:1). David's baser appetites had conquered his reason and sense of duty, and ironically, he had usurped his own authority to be king and establish an enduring dynasty (2 Sam 12:10–12).

Similarly, as Adam fell by listening to his wife (Gen 3:17), so too did Solomon fall by letting his wives turn his heart (1 Kgs 11:3; cf. Neh 13:26). Whereas at first Solomon had built a temple for God (1 Kgs 6–8), later in his reign he built high places for foreign gods (1 Kgs 11:7–8).[29] Whereas previously Solomon had used his wisdom to bring justice to his people (1 Kgs 3:16–28), later he used it to amass wealth and power for himself (e.g., 1 Kgs 10:14–29).

Knowledge of sin

Similar to how Adam had been made aware of the irreversible consequences of his sin, David was notified that Bathsheba was pregnant (2 Sam 11:5), and similar to how Adam had attempted to remedy his shameful nakedness by clothing himself, David attempted to remedy his shameful sin by having Uriah killed (2 Sam 11:6–25).[30]

Solomon also sought to remedy the consequences of his apostasy by seeking to kill Jeroboam, the future king of the northern ten tribes (1 Kgs 11:9–13, 40).

29. In fact, according to 2 Kgs 23:13, Solomon built his abominations on the Olivet Ridge east of Zion, which was topographically higher than Zion.

30. Like Adam, David was naked when he committed his sin. This is marked out as David's primary sin in 1 Kgs 15:5 (curiously leaving absent the matter of the census; cf. 1 Sam 24).

Curse

As God had rebuked Adam for his sin, so too did Nathan rebuke David for his (2 Sam 12:7–9). As David demanded a four-fold payment for the crime he heard in Nathan's parable (2 Sam 12:5–6), four of his children would be killed for his own crime: Bathsheba's child (2 Sam 12:14–23), Amnon (2 Sam 13:23–29), Absalom (2 Sam 18:15),[31] and Adonijah (1 Kgs 2:13–25).[32] As Adam had become the father of a murderous son, so too has David become the father of murderous children (2 Sam 13:23–29).[33]

Solomon was cursed by knowing that the kingdom would be torn away from him and given to his servant (1 Kgs 11:11), something which the book of Ecclesiastes mourns (Eccl 2:18–21; 6:1–2).

Forgiveness

Nevertheless, as God had forgiven Adam, so too did God forgive David and ensure him the survival of his line (2 Sam 7:13; 1 Kgs 11:29–39; cf. Ps 32:1).

31. There are several thematic parallels between Ham's sin against Noah and Absalom's sin against David. For example, both slept with their father's wife/wives in an attempt to usurp authority, and Ham's descendant was cursed while Absalom died without children. Also, it is interesting to note how David was banished eastward from Jerusalem similar to how Adam and Eve were banished eastward of Eden (Gen 3:24; 2 Sam 15:23). This same eastward movement will be repeated by Jesus, the last Adam and new David, on the night he will be banished as if he were a sinner (Jn 18:1).

32. The tabulation of children could be different. For example, another one of David's children, Tamar, will be raped (by Amnon, whom Absalom will kill). If this is considered the female equivalent to being killed (note: she does not appear to have remarried, and thus never had descendants; 2 Sam 13:20), then Bathsheba's child forms part of the "sheep" that David took from Uriah (2 Sam 11:11), for which he paid with the death of three sons and the rape of his daughter. Whatever the case may have been, the point is the poetic justice of David's unwitting self-condemnation.

33. Notably, bloodshed was the reason why David was prohibited from building the temple (1 Chr 22:8; 28:3).

God did not tear the whole kingdom away from Solomon during his own life, but rather waited until his son was on the throne to do so, and spared him one tribe (1 Kgs 11:12–13).

4. Division (2 Sam 13–2 Kgs 23)

Division

David's sin with Bathsheba was followed by a division within his own family, including rape, murder, and eventually political rebellion (2 Sam 13–18). This, however, was simply the precursor to the much more important division that would play out after Solomon's death: the division of the Israelite kingdom into north and south (1 Kgs 12).

King Jeroboam began his reign by essentially reenacting the golden calf episode of Exodus 32: he made golden calves, declared that they were the ones who brought Israel out of Egypt, and observed a festival (1 Kgs 12:28–33; cf. Exod 32:4–6). The biblical verdict for both stories was the same: it was a great sin (2 Kgs 17:21; cf. Exod 32:21, 30–31). Jeroboam even named his sons Nadab and Abijah, eerily reminiscent of the sons of Aaron who rebelled against Moses and were consumed by fire from the LORD (1 Kgs 14:1, 20; cf. Lev 10:1–2).[34]

Persecution

The northern and southern kingdoms, the former of which was clearly the more dominant with regard to land and population, lived in near-perpetual conflict, often with the northern kingdom exercising direct or indirect authority over the southern kingdom (e.g., 1 Kgs 11:39).

34. For the parallels between Jeroboam and the golden calf episode, cf. Frisch, "Exodus Motif," 16–17.

Cities

Under the leadership of king Jeroboam, the cities of Shechem and Peniel were built in the mountainous region of Ephraim (1 Kgs 12:25), and idolatrous centers of worship at Bethel and Dan were established as direct competitors with Jerusalem and the temple cult there (1 Kgs 12:26–33).[35] Jeroboam's successors continued to build cities such as Samaria and Jericho, all of which represented their rebellion and functioned as anti-Jerusalems (1 Kgs 16:24, 34). After Israel was carried into captivity and the land was resettled with foreigners, they built new cities where they made sacrifices to their gods (2 Kgs 17:29–33).

Apostasy; inter-marriage

Both kingdoms perpetuated their spiritual idolatry. Every king of Israel followed Jeroboam's idolatry, and it would not be until the reign of king Josiah of Judah, after Israel had already been taken into captivity, that the golden calves were destroyed (2 Kg 23:15). Similarly, even when the book of Kings provides a positive evaluation of the kings of Judah, on most occasions it adds that they did not remove the high places and that the people continued to offer sacrifices on them.[36]

The southern kingdom was constantly drawn away from following the Lord, and the majority of its kings were evil.[37] Although there was something of a revival after the fall of the northern kingdom, by the end of the southern kingdom's existence they had become as wicked as the northern kingdom (Jer 3:6–10; Ezek 23:11–21). Judah had been unfaithful to the Lord and was called a whore on several occasions (e.g., Isa 1:21; Jer

35. Notice the repeated refrain throughout 1–2 Kgs that places the blame at the feet of Israel's first king, Jeroboam: "Jeroboam the son of Nebat, which he made Israel to sin" (e.g., 2 Kgs 10:29; cf. 17:21–31).

36. First Kgs 15:14; 22:43; 2 Kgs 12:3; 14:4; 15:4, 35. The only exceptions are Hezekiah and Josiah (2 Kgs 18:4; 23:4–20), who are regarded as the best kings of Judah (2 Kgs 18:5; 23:25).

37. Of Judah's twenty kings, only eight were righteous in God's eyes: Asa, Jehoshaphat, Joash, Amaziah, Azariah (Uzziah), Jotham, Hezekiah, and Josiah.

2:20; Ezek 16:15–17).[38] As Cain had built the city of Enoch as a type of anti-Eden, both kingdoms built altars and shrines on the high places that functioned as spiritual anti-Jerusalems (e.g., 1 Kgs 11:6–8; 2 Kgs 17:9–12; Jer 19:4–5;).[39] Like the antediluvians, the land was filled with bloodshed (2 Kgs 21:16; 24:3–4; cf. Ezek 9:9). According to Isaiah, the most fitting city name for the land's inhabitants was not Jerusalem and Judah, but rather Sodom and Gomorrah (Isa 1:10). Instead of yielding the sweet grapes of justice and righteousness, the people had yielded the wild grapes of bloodshed and outcry (Isa 5:3–4, 7).

Prophet; preacher of righteousness

God sent many prophets to his people (2 Kgs 17:13), of whom Elijah and Elisha are perhaps the most famous (1 Kgs 17–2 Kgs 13).[40] He also sent some prophets whose writings form part of the Hebrew Scriptures (cf. Neh 9:30). God had appointed Jeremiah over nations and kingdoms with a similar authority that he had given to those with whom he had made his covenants; however, instead of commanding him to fill the earth with God's glory, he was commanded to uproot, tear down, destroy, and overthrow (Jer 1:10).[41]

Affliction; 'crying out'

Similar to how the Egyptians had afflicted the Israelites by placing burdens on them as they were making Pithom and Rameses,

38. Ezekiel goes so far as to describe Judah as Sodom's sister (Ezek 16:48-49, 56; 23:31, 33; cf. Jer 23:14).

39. Jeremiah 7:30 and 32:34 say that the temple in Jerusalem itself had been infiltrated.

40. As several authors have noted, the Omride dynasty forms the chiastic centerpiece of the book of Kgs, with the ministries of Elijah and Elisha taking center stage (Dorsey, *Literary Structure*, 142–43; Waltke, *Old Testament Theology*, 704). Thus, the conflict between Elijah and Elisha and the wicked northern kingdom is the hermeneutical key for interpreting the book as a whole.

41. Two other verbs are used—to build and plant (Jer 1:10)—, but the emphasis falls heavily on the destructive side of things.

Solomon placed burdens on the Israelites to fulfill his construction projects in and around Jerusalem (1 Kgs 11:28).[42] Prophets like Jeremiah 'cried out' because of the affliction and violence in the land (e.g., Jer 20:8).

5. Judgment[43] (2 Kgs 17; 24–25)

Near the end of the southern kingdom's existence, its most wicked king, Manasseh, ruled for fifty-five years (2 Kgs 21:1). He filled Jerusalem with very much innocent blood (2 Kgs 21:16; 24:3-4; cf. Ezek 9:9), thereby evoking the horrendous situation just before the flood when man's only thought was to do evil continually, and violence filled the earth (Gen 6:5, 13).

Chaos; flood

It should be no wonder, therefore, that the prophets used flood and chaos imagery to convey God's judgment on Judah.[44] The glory of the LORD, manifested in the form of a cloud that once had filled the temple, has been taken away (Ezek 8–10). Indeed, the temple itself was destroyed and the city's walls were knocked down (2 Kgs 25:1–17). As the LORD had rejected Saul, he now rejects all of Israel's descendants (2 Kgs 17:18–23) and even Jerusalem itself (2 Kgs 23:27). As the earth had been 'formless' and 'void' in the beginning, so too did the LORD make Judah 'formless' and 'void'

42. It is ironic to note that the individual that Solomon placed in charge of these burdens was Jeroboam, the future king of the northern ten tribes of Israel (1 Kgs 11:26–40).

43. Cf. Childs, "Enemy from the North," whose thesis could be seen as complimentary to the argument made here. He argues that the root "shake" (Heb: רעשׁ, *ra'ash*) "appears to have developed into a technical term for the final shaking of the world at the return of chaos" and that this idea fused with the "enemy-from-the-north" tradition ("Enemy from the North," 197). The concept of "shaking" comes into prominence during this cycle.

44. Isaiah 24:1–3, 18-20; Jer 4:23–28; Zeph 1:2–6. Flood language is also used to convey the northern kingdom's invasion by the Assyrians (Isa 8:7-8; 17:12-13; Amos 8:8; 9:5). Also, God sent similar plagues to the northern kingdom as he had sent to Egypt (Amos 4:8).

(Jer 4:23–26).[45] It seems as if God had renounced the covenant he made with David (Ps 89:37–51). God has torn down his ordered vineyard and allowed chaos to overcome it (Isa 5:5–6). At the Day of the LORD, invading armies will turn Edenic Jerusalem into a waste wilderness (Joel 2:3).

Exile; expulsion

Already during Solomon's reign, Israel was threatened with being 'sent' from the land if they would forsake God (1 Kgs 9:6–7), as Adam and Eve had been 'sent' from the garden (Gen 3:23). It was due to Manasseh's sins that the southern kingdom went into exile,[46] the story of which is recounted in 2 Kings 23:26–25:26 (esp. 25:21).[47] God has removed Judah—even Jerusalem itself—as he had removed Israel (2 Kgs 23:27). Some fled to Egypt while most others were taken captive to Babylon (2 Kgs 24:1–25:21, 26). Instead of Israel possessing the land from the Nile to the Euphrates, it is Babylon, the emblematic kingdom of chaos, that does so (2 Kgs 24:7). It was during Israel's exile that her imprecatory psalms reached their climax in praying for their enemies' babies—i.e., the Edomites—to be dashed against the rock (Ps 137).

Deliverance of righteous remnant

While it is true that Amos went so far as to imply the destruction of even the remnant of Israel (Amos 9:1–4), this must be qualified by his other statements that a remnant would indeed survive (Amos 5:3; 6:9–10). His point, however, was to be taken seriously: God's anger was such that it would appear as if he would completely

45. For the many parallels between Gen 1 and Jer 4:23–26, cf. Fishbane, "Jeremiah *IV* 23-26"; Craigie et al., *Jeremiah 1–25*, 81. Interestingly, this judgment of exile also forms an *inclusio* with the beginning of the Abraham cycle: Abraham was taken out of Babylon and his descendants were ultimately exiled back there; cf. Messmer, "Possible Chiastic Center."

46. Second Kgs 23:26–27; 24:3–4; Jer 15:4; Ezek 12:19.

47. For the story of the northern kingdom's exile, cf. 2 Kgs 17:6–23.

annihilate Israel, and even the small surviving remnant would be meaningless to the survival of the nation as a whole.[48]

Many Jews would be killed by the flood waters of the Assyrian and Babylonian armies, and yet God preserved a remnant for himself.[49] In fact, in a stunning act of reversal, Isaiah 13–14 predicted the downfall of Babylon like that of Sodom and Gomorrah, and that God would once again make Israel 'rest' in her land (Isa 14:1–3).[50]

48. Hasel, *The Remnant*, 392.

49. Second Kgs 19:30–31; Isa 10:22–23; Jer 24:4–10; 29:10–14.

50. There is a clear play on the theme of 'rest' in Isa 13:20–14:4, which employs four different Hebrew words that are used six times altogether; cf. Wegner, *A Student's Guide*, 166 n. 42.

Chapter 7: Zerubbabel, Representing the Remnant of Judah

Ezra–Nehemiah

After the reigns of twenty kings of Judah and seventy years in captivity, God recreated again through Zerubbabel and the remnant community. In the three waves of Jews that Scripture records to have returned to the Promised Land, four figures are especially prominent: Zerubbabel and Joshua in the first wave,[1] Ezra in the second, and Nehemiah in the third. These waves spanned nearly a century, and thus we find that, similar to the David cycle, some stages are quite protracted and involve repetition. Of the tribe of Judah, only a remnant had remained faithful to God, and it is this remnant that now represents God to the world.[2] The geographic focus has reduced from the southern kingdom to the city of Jerusalem and its surrounding environs.

1. These two are frequently mentioned together (e.g., Ezra 3:8; Neh 12:1; Hag 1:1).

2. Only the tribes of Judah, Benjamin, and Levi are mentioned as returning from exile (e.g., Ezra 1:5; 10:9; Neh 11:4). Benjamin is essentially assumed into Judah and Levi must be present in order to have a valid priesthood. Only those of these three tribes are said to repopulate Jerusalem (Neh 11:4, 7, 10, 15). They represent the "remnant" (2 Kgs 19:30–31; Ezra 9:8, 13–15; Neh 1:2–3).

1. Creation (Ezra–Neh)

Creation from chaos

Because of their sin, the dreadful curse of Deuteronomy 28:36–68 had overtaken Judah: the temple has been reduced to ashes, the city wall has been torn down, king Jehoiachin has been taken captive, king Zedekiah has been humiliated and his line has ended, and the people have been taken into exile (2 Kgs 24:12; 25:7–11). Those who were not exiled to Babylon fled to Egypt (2 Kgs 25:26). It is from this darkness that God recreates, but it is a slow process that spans over a century:[3] Ezra 1–6 recounts the first return from exile as well as the rebuilding of the temple (Ezra 6:14–15),[4] Ezra 7–10 recounts the second return and a public act of repentance and return to the LORD, and Nehemiah 1–13 recounts the rebuilding of the wall around Jerusalem and a covenant renewal ceremony.[5]

Both before and after the exile, God's prophets spoke of a new exodus in which God would bring his people—often identified as a remnant—out of exile and restore them to their land, often using imagery reminiscent of the first exodus from Egypt.[6] This new exodus also evokes the times after Noah: as God had sworn never to send a flood again, he swore again never to revoke his covenant with Israel (Isa 54:9–10; cf. Gen 9:11–16). Some prophets even said that God would make Jerusalem and its surrounding environs like Eden (Isa 51:3; 58:11; Jer 31:12; Ezek 36:35).[7] The seventy years of

3. The first return happened in 538 BC, the second in 458 BC, and the third in 444 BC.

4. It is this remnant that God will regard as good and establish them in the land once again (Jer 24).

5. A previous, unsuccessful, attempt at rebuilding (parts of) the wall is recorded in Ezra 4:6–23. Bruce Waltke, summarizing arguments others have made, argues that Ezra's departure from Babylon and entrance into Judah are a new Exodus and new Conquest, respectively (*Old Testament Theology*, 139–41).

6. Isaiah 10:24–27; 11:15–16; 37:32; 51:9–11; Jer 16:14–15; 23:7–8; 24:4–7; 29:10–14; Ezek 36:22–38; 37:1–14; Joel 2:28–32.

7. For more garden-like language, cf. Isa 30:23–26; 35:5–7; 41:17–20.

exile which Jeremiah had prophesied have now been completed (Jer 25:12; 29:10; Zech 1:12–17; 7:5), and the temple vessels that Nebuchadnezzar had taken to Babylon were returned by Cyrus (Ezra 1:7–11; 5:14–15; cf. 2 Kgs 24:12–13).

Some interesting contrasts can be seen with Israel's first exodus from Egypt. Whereas Pharaoh was against letting God's people go (e.g., Exod 5:2), Cyrus was the one supporting and financing their return (Ezra 1:2–4). Although God had hardened Pharaoh's heart (e.g., Exod 4:21), he stirred up Cyrus' spirit (Ezra 1:1). As the Israelites had left Egypt with plunder (Exod 3:22; 12:35–36), the Jews were leaving Babylon with gifts from Cyrus (Ezra 1:2–4; 6:3–5).

While there is no doubt that God is recreating once again, there is also no doubt that there is something still quite wrong: their temple is a mere shadow of its former glory (Ezra 3:12–13; Hag 2:3), they have no king but only a governor (e.g., Neh 5:14), the remnant have not returned as freedmen but as slaves (Ezra 9:8–9; Neh 9:36), and they are being constantly hounded by enemies.[8] In fact, the prophets already are prophesying about a better future: a more glorious temple (Hag 2:3–9; Zech 6:12–15), a restored king/messiah,[9] a true shepherd (Mic 5:2–4), freedom from slavery (Zech 9:11), and peace and blessing (Ezek 34:25–30; 36:35). Creation during this cycle, therefore, is imperfect at best.[10]

8. For example, Ezra 4:1–6; 5:3–4; Neh 2:19–20; 4:1–3, 7–8; 6:1–14. In the case of Nehemiah, there is a fusion of opposition from Samaria (Sanballat: Neh 2:10), Ammon (Tobiah: Neh 2:10), and Arabia (Geshem: Neh 2:19; 6:6), and thus they are surrounded by ancient and current enemies. Josephus adds that many Jews were killed by these enemies (to which he adds the Moabites and other inhabitants of Syria; cf. *Antiq.* 11:174–75).

9. Ezekiel 34:23–24; Zech 3:8–9 (cf. Jer 23:5; 33:15); 6:12–14.

10. Consider also the many sins that Israel falls prey to during this time (e.g., Hag 1:3–11).

Creation battle

The Samaritans attempted to stop the building of the temple and the city walls, but they were unsuccessful (Ezra 4–6; Neh 4; 6). False prophets and political foes arose and tried to make Nehemiah afraid (Neh 6:14, 19), but they failed as well.

God's Spirit

Once again, God's 'Spirit' is dwelling with his people (Hag 2:5). The books of Ezra and Nehemiah speak of God's hand being with them, which suggests God's sovereign presence.[11]

God's word

There does not appear to be any discernable emphasis on God's word in this cycle.

Temple

In fulfillment of Isaiah's prophecy (Isa 44:28), Cyrus commanded that the Jewish temple be rebuilt, sent the original temple vessels back with those returning to their homeland, and helped to fund the costs (Ezra 1:2–4, 7–11; 6:3–5). Thus, as with previous cycles, the temple was rebuilt once again with plunder taken from the Babylonians and Persians (Ezra 6:3–5). Although construction was temporarily halted (Ezra 4:24), it was eventually finished thanks to the prophetic ministries of Haggai and Zechariah. The remnant community celebrated the Passover again (Ezra 6:19–22), and they celebrated the Festival of Booths as they had not done so since Joshua's conquest of Canaan (Neh 8:17). The remnant once again worshiped God in his temple with a restored priesthood (Ezra 10:18–44).

11. For example, Ezra 7:6, 9, 28; Neh 2:8; cf. 1 Kgs 18:46; 2 Kgs 3:15.

Rest

As God had made Adam 'rest' in the garden of Eden, he had promised to make Israel 'rest' again in their land (Isa 14:1–3; Ezek 37:14), which seems to have been fulfilled, at least partially, with the return from captivity.

2. Man (Ezra–Neh; Hag; Zech 1–6)

Election

Although Judah's king, Jehoiachin, had been released from prison and given a relative degree of freedom and honor in the Babylonian court (2 Kgs 25:27–30), he had already been cast out of God's presence like the throwing away of a signet ring (Jer 22:24–30).[12] Instead, God had put on a new signet ring, Zerubbabel, who, in addition to being a descendant of David (1 Chr 3:17–19, cf. v. 10), was the branch and servant that God had chosen.[13] In addition, God raised up Joshua the high priest (Zech 3:1–5; 6:9–15), thereby restoring the Zadokite priesthood to its former place of glory (1 Chr 6:15). In fact, according to 1 Chronicles 6:1–15, there were twelve high priests from Aaron to the building of the first temple, and eleven from the first temple until the exile, thereby making Joshua the twelfth high priest from the building of the first temple to the building of the second, which gives a balanced structure to the entire high priestly chronology.[14] Together, Zerubbabel and Joshua were the two olive trees and anointed ones who stood by the Lord of the whole earth (Zech 4:11–14).[15]

12. Sheshbazzar was only a prince of Judah or governor of the land (Ezra 1:8; 5:14). At most, he was the ruler of the Judean province when Cyrus took power, and at any rate his Babylonian name may have made him a foreigner (however, Zerubbabel is also called governor; e.g., Hag 1:1, 14).

13. Haggai 2:20–23; Zech 3:8; 6:12–13; cf. Is 11:1; Zech 4:1–10. For these connections with messianic themes, cf. Isa 41:8; 42:1; 50:10; 52:13; 53:11. It is important to note that Zech 4:1–14 is the fourth of seven visions in the book of Zech, thereby making it the central vision around which the whole book is constructed.

14. Miller and Hayes, *History of Ancient Israel*, 519.

15. Ralph Smith says it "probably" refers to them (*Micah–Malachi*, 205).

Thus there was restoration of both kingly and priestly functions of Jewish society and religion.[16]

Formed outside; 'go forth'

Except for a few of the elderly (Ezra 3:12–13; Hag 2:3), the remnant generation that returned to Judea was born and raised in Babylon. Thus, they function as a kind of corporate Abraham *redivivus*: as he had been formed in Babylon, so too had they; as he had gone forth to the Promised Land, so too did they.

Mixed multitude

Nehemiah writes that foreigners—specifically Ammonites and Moabites—were in the midst of the congregation of Israel, and thus called them a 'mixed' multitude (Neh 13:3; cf. Exod 12:38). As has been seen in previous cycles, this will be a major contribution to their downfall.

Mountain and garden

The remnant's destination was the mountain-city of Jerusalem, (Ezra 1:2, 5; Ezek 34:26), and their first task was to rebuild the temple, thereby evoking the garden theme once more (Ezra 3:1–13; 6:13–18; Ezek 34:25–31; 36:35). Using mountain and garden imagery, Ezekiel prophesied of a future time in which God would restore the fortunes of Israel: God would take a sprig from the old cedar tree and place it on the high and lofty mountain, where it would become a world tree that offered food and shelter for every bird (Ezek 17:22–24). The old cedar tree symbolized the old Davidic empire, and thus the sprig signified the reestablishment of

16. The high priest (Joshua) and governor (Zerubbabel) often are mentioned together. In fact, the book of Hag is addressed to them both, and Zech 4:14 calls them "the two anointed ones who stand by the Lord of the whole earth."

the Davidic dynasty on the only mountain of any significance to the remnant community: Jerusalem.[17]

Diving blessing and commands

Under the leadership of Ezra,[18] the remnant celebrated covenant renewal ceremonies (Neh 8–10, esp. 9:38–10:27), thereby evoking the blessing and commands of previous cycles. It is important to note, however, that various prophets before, during, and after the exile began to look forward to a new covenant in which God would put his law in his people's hearts and give them his Spirit once again.[19]

3. Fall (Ezra–Neh; Hag 1; Mal)

As with previous cycles, it is difficult to identify one specific sin, but there are clear indicators that the remnant community was not faithful to God or the covenant renewal stipulations.

Not vigilant

Instead of focusing on building the temple, the remnant community built their own houses (Hag 1:2–4, 9). The Ammonite Tobiah, who apparently had married a Jewish woman, had gained great influence in Jerusalem, and many of the nobles extolled his deeds to Nehemiah (Neh 6:17–19). In fact, during Nehemiah's absence, a priest had even given him a room in the temple (Neh 13:4–7). The remnant community was not focused on following God, but rather on seeking a comfortable life and making alliances with powerful, but corrupt, foreigners.

17. Stordalen, *Echoes of Eden*, 172–73. The fact that the cedar tree produces fruit suggests that Ezekiel had fused the idea of the cedar world tree with that of the vine.

18. Ezra was a descendant of Seraiah, apparently the high priest just before the Babylonian exile (1 Chr 6:10–15; Ezra 7:1–6).

19. Jeremiah 31:31–34; 32:36–41; Ezek 11:17–20; 16:59–62; 20:37; 34:25; 36:22–32; 37:24–28; 39:29; Hos 2:14–23. It is interesting to note the connection between covenant and eating in Jer 31:29–30.

Woman; deception/seduction; usurpation

The remnant community has returned to its old ways: their hearts were as hard as a diamond, and they continued to oppress the widow, orphan, foreigner, and poor (Zech 7:8–12). The wealthier Jews enslaved poorer ones because they could not repay their debts (Neh 5:1–8), and they all failed to keep themselves separate from the surrounding nations, with some marrying their women (Ezra 9:1–2; 10:18–44). Even some priests and Levites, including some of Joshua's sons, were found to have married foreign women (Ezra 10:18–24). During Nehemiah's absence, the remnant community again departed from the way: they promoted syncretism, neglected temple duties, profaned the Sabbath, and married foreign women (Neh 13). Malachi prophesied against many evils that the community was committing: polluting offerings (Mal 1:6–14), a corrupt priesthood (Mal 2:1–9), spiritual and marital adultery (Mal 2:10–16), social evils (Mal 3:5), and laxity in paying tithes to support the temple (Mal 3:6–9).

Knowledge of sin

The remnant community became aware of their sin when Ezra tore his clothes, pulled out his hair, fasted until evening, and prayed aloud weeping (Ezra 9:3–5; 10:1–4). Similarly, Nehemiah led the remnant community in another act of public confession including fasting, sackcloth, and dirt on their heads (Neh 9).

Curse

Because the remnant had been lax in rebuilding God's temple, God was withholding rain from heaven and all the blessings that it brings (Hag 1:10–11). More seriously, God was no longer regarding their offerings (Mal 2:13).

Forgiveness

Led by Ezra and Nehemiah, Israel publicly repented of their sin (Ezra 9–10; Neh 9). The wealthier Jews showed their repentance by cancelling the debts of the poorer Jewish borrowers (Neh 5:9–13). So that God would not completely destroy his people, he promised to send them Elijah, who would restore them to his ways (Mal 4:5–6).

4. Division

The Old Testament does not relate much information regarding the subsequent division of the remnant, but post-biblical texts sufficiently demonstrate the matter.

Division

The Jews struggled as they lived as slaves in the Promised Land under Persian and Greek rule. During the mid-second century BC, Judaism fractured into several distinct groups as it sought to respond to the influence of Greek society and religion and the persecution brought on by Antiochus IV Epiphanes (1 Macc 1–4). Pharisees, Sadducees, and Essenes all trace their origins back to this time, with Zealots, Herodians, and other splinter groups cropping up sometime during Roman domination in the mid-first century BC.[20]

Persecution

Each sect considered itself the faithful remnant and sought to defeat the others through dialogue, debate, political maneuvering, and even violence. However, like Eli during the time of the judges and the religious establishment shortly before the exile, those who were supposed to be the most righteous were actually the most corrupt. Like Adam, they sought to cover their spiritual nakedness with the man-made cloth of self-righteousness. Persecution reached its climax when the Jews, led by the various sects, persecuted and killed God's Son, Jesus Christ (e.g., Mark 12:1–8; Luke 4:28–29; John 8:59).

20. Josephus, *War* 2.119–66.

Cities

Unable to build new cities due to their servile condition under the Romans, groups such as the Pharisees and Sadducees attempted to build names for themselves: they sought public recognition for their religious practices, desired the best seats at religious and social gatherings, and enjoyed being recognized as superior to others (Matt 23:5–7). Although they built and decorated the tombs of Israel's prophets and other righteous men, it was to their own condemnation, since they, too, would have persecuted them had they had the chance (Matt 23:29–31). In contrast, pious Jews such as Ana looked to God in prayer (Luke 2:37), and humble Joseph and Mary 'call' their son Jesus and Immanuel (Matt 1:21–23).

Apostasy; inter-marriage

As has been noted above, some Jews renounced their faith in the face of Hellenistic pressure and persecution (1 Macc 1:11–16, 45–55). Entire Greek cities had been established in the Promised Land (e.g., the Decapolis; cf. Mark 7:31), and some people were raising pigs in the land (Mark 5:11–13). Jewish rulers such as Antipater and Herod were half-Edomites,[21] and commoners such as Timothy's mother Eunice married Greeks (Acts 16:1; cf. 2 Tim 1:5).

Prophet; preacher of righteousness

As God had sent Elijah to preach to northern Israel shortly before its collapse and judgment, he sent John the Baptist to preach against all Israel, especially against the religious elite (e.g., Matt 3:7–12). Comparing the lives and messages of Elijah and John the Baptist, it is clear that John the Baptist was a kind of Elijah *redividus* (Matt 11:11–15; cf. Mal 4:5–6).

Affliction; 'crying out'

Pious Jews like Simeon and Anna were waiting for God's salvation and prayed for it earnestly (Luke 2:22–38). Mary's and Zechariah's

21. Josephus, *War* 1.123; *Antiq* 14.403 (cf. m. Sota 7:8).

prayers in Luke 1:46–55 and 67–79 are filled with references to the humble and afflicted state of God's people and is a way of crying out to God for deliverance.

5. Judgment

This cycle's judgment crosses over into the next, but only because of God's patience and willingness to give his people a chance to repent.

Chaos; flood

In judgment for their rejection of God's chosen Messiah (see below), God brought the flood of the Roman army on the Jews. The first tidal wave came in c. AD 66–70 and was well-documented by ancient authors such as Josephus (cf. *War*). The second tidal wave came in c. AD 132–135 during the Bar Kochba Revolt. Until the twentieth century, the Jews did not have control over the Promised Land (and their control is still not complete even today), and they are still unable to rebuild the temple and offer sacrifices.

Exile; expulsion

Because the Jews tore down the temple of Jesus' body (see below), God tore down their temple in c. AD 70. With Jesus being identified as the true Israelite (see below), God sent ethnic Israel into permanent exile.

Deliverance of righteous remnant

Despite wide-spread rejection by the Jews, not all rejected Jesus as God's Messiah. God has preserved a remnant for himself (Rom 11:5–7; cf. 9:27): Paul himself was a Jew (Rom 11:1), as were many thousands of the first followers of the Way (e.g., Acts 2:41; 4:4; 6:7), and some of the apostles such as Peter had a special ministry to the Jews (Gal 2:7).

Chapter 8: The One Man, Jesus Christ, Representing All Mankind

In the fullness of time (Gal 4:4; cf. Heb 9:26), God sent his Son, in whom all of God's promises are yes and amen (2 Cor 1:20). All history—biblical and cosmic—is united in him (Eph 1:10). Whereas Adam, Noah, the patriarchs, Moses, Joshua, David, and the remnant were faithless,[1] Jesus was faithful. All disobeyed and failed, but this was God's plan, in order that he might have mercy on all (Rom 11:32) and in order to prepare the world for the coming of God's chosen Messiah, who was the right person, doing the right things, and coming at the right time and place. Two factors make this cycle different from the previous ones: 1) Because of Jesus's faithfulness instead of faithlessness, many of the themes are antithetical to those of previous cycles.[2] 2) Because Jesus is the head of the Church and has given to her his Spirit, much of what can be said about Jesus also applies to the Church. Thus, a separate

1. Isaiah 43:27–28 speaks of the failure of (some of) the patriarchs, Moses and Aaron, and the kings; cf. Watts, *Isaiah 34–66*, 688.

2. This closely aligns with Irenaeus' doctrine of recapitulation. As John Lawson summarizes the matter, Jesus 'went through all the experiences of Adam but with the opposite result' (*Biblical Theology of Saint Irenaeus*, 143). Cf. Irenaeus, *AH* 3:21:10; 5:23:2.

section is found at the end of each stage, highlighting how Christ's ministry is translated to the Church.

The geographic focus has reduced from Jerusalem and its environs to one man, Jesus Christ, and then opens up again in his Church to include the whole world (e.g., Matt 28:18–20). He is not simply the king of one nation, but rather of all.[3]

1. Creation

Creation from chaos

God's people were severely afflicted and had been so for quite some time (Luke 1:46–55, 67–79). They were slaves in their own land (Luke 2:1; 3:1), and wicked Caiaphas was the high priest.[4] Wicked king Herod, himself of Edomite/Idumean descent,[5] was sitting on the throne, and similar to Pharaoh, he would rather slaughter innocent babies than have his rule threatened (Matt 2:16–18). Darkness was in the land, but a great light was beginning to shine (Matt 4:12–17). Jesus will complete this recreation upon his death, which was a new exodus (Luke 9:31).

Creation battle

With Jesus's birth, God was liberating his people from bondage and conquering their evil foes (Luke 1:46–55, 68–75; 2:29–32).[6] As God had defeated the monsters of chaos before, now he conquers the ultimate monster of chaos: the devil (Rev 12:1–9). Jesus has entered the strong man's house and bound him, and subsequently has plundered his house (Mark 3:27). The serpent who had successfully seduced Adam and Eve to sin in the garden was powerless when tempting the true Adam, whether it was in a

3. Genesis 49:10; Ps 2:8; Dan 7:13–14; cf. Rev 5:9.

4. Luke 3:2; cf. John 11:49–51; Acts 5:17–18; 9:1–2.

5. Josephus, *Antiq*. 14.403; cf. m. Sot 7:8.

6. Second exodus language is used here (Nolland, *Luke*, 65). Also, Herod fulfills the role of a second Pharaoh in his attempt to kill all the male babies, with the promised child barely escaping death (Matt 2:13–18).

desert (Matt 4:1–11) or a garden (Matt 26:36–46). The arrival of Jesus signified the destruction of evil, which is cast in cosmic terminology (Matt 24:1–39; Acts 2:19–20).[7] Whereas Jesus' enemies had asserted that Jesus was an agent of the serpent (Matt 12:24), it was they who were the serpent's spiritual sons (John 8:44), and thus Jesus's victorious debates with the religious leaders and his casting out of demons were enactments of God's victory over the forces of chaos (Luke 10:18). One day, the last enemy, death, will be destroyed (1 Cor 15:25–26).

God's Spirit

God's Spirit indwelt Jesus fully (Isa 11:2; Matt 3:16) and was with him at his birth (Luke 1:35),[8] baptism (Matt 3:16), ministry (Matt 12:28), and resurrection (Rom 1:4). Jesus' words are Spirit and life (John 6:63).

God's word

Jesus' teaching in the Sermon on the Mount fulfills God's original Ten Words which he spoke to Israel (Matt 5:17–20). His word was just as authoritative as God's (e.g., Matt 5:21–22), and he expected his followers to obey him (Matt 7:24–29).

7. It is important to note the correspondence between the rending of the temple veil (Matt 27:51) and the rending of Christ's flesh (Heb 10:20).

8. It is possible that Mary is being stylized as the new ark of the covenant, playing off the themes found in 2 Sam 6. John Nolland says of the connections between this text and Lk 1: "Echoes of 2 Sam 6:2–19 are to be found in vv 41, 43, 44, and possibly v 56. Except for the last, what we have is a taking up of language that expresses a paradigmatic response to that which marks the presence and activity of God. If the last be granted (v 56; cf 2 Sam 6:11), then we must go further and say that this taking up of paradigmatic responses has been artistically carried through by treating the presence of Mary (or the unborn Jesus) as equivalent to the presence of the ark of the covenant" (*Luke*, 74).

Temple

Whereas previously God's temple had taken the shape of creation, tabernacle, and temple, now it has become the body of his Son, Jesus (John 2:19–22).[9] As God's presence had filled the tabernacle and temple, so too did the Spirit overshadow Mary (Luke 1:35).

Rest

As God had rested after he finished his work of creation, Jesus rested after his work was finished on the cross (Heb 1:3; Jn 5:17; 19:30).[10]

The Church

This new creation which the Father has brought about by the Son has been passed on to the Church through her sharing in the Spirit. Thus, as God's original creation can be described as overcoming chaos, darkness, and death, now God overcomes Satan to bring Christians out of the domain of darkness and into the

9. According to Patristic interpretation, the temple that Moses saw when he ascended Mount Sinai was none other than the Son himself (e.g., Gregory of Nyssa, *Life of Moses*, 174).

10. The fact that both restings took place on the seventh day ought not to be overlooked. Warren Gage has noticed some striking parallels between the original creation in Gen 1 and Jesus' passion week: "On the first day of the redemptive week, the Light of the World approached the temple from the direction of the eastern sunrise (cf. Matt 21:9; Ps 118:26–27). During the week the Word of God spoke daily in the temple (Luke 19:47), entering into creative combat with the religious and political leaders, who represented, according to John, the darkness of original creation (John 1:5, cf. 13:30). On the sixth day of Passion Week, the Word surveyed His redemptive work and pronounced it finished (John 19:30, cf. Gen 2:3), resting on the sabbath day in the rest of death (John 19:31). This is the old creation redemptively reenacted in the new creation" (*Gospel of Genesis*, 22). Reflecting on the phrase "the Light of the World approached the temple" he adds, "Since creation is often described as a dwelling place God has built (cf. Ps 104; Job 9:8; Isa 40:22) the temple represents the cosmos (cf. Ps 78:69; John 2:21; 1 Cor 6:19). The temple (as a dwelling place of the Spirit) is consequently a metaphor equally apt for macrocosmic and microcosmic expression" (*Gospel of Genesis*, 22 n. 20).

Son's kingdom (Col 1:13). Although Satan has brought spiritual darkness to humanity, God overcomes this darkness by his Son and speaks light into our hearts (2 Cor 4:4–6; cf. Eph 5:14). As God had breathed life into man in the garden (Gen 2:7), and as Ezekiel had prophesied about God breathing on dry bones to make them come alive (Ezek 37:9), now Jesus breathes on his disciples to give them the Holy Spirit (John 20:21–22). It is no coincidence that the coming of the Spirit in Acts 2:2 is described as a "mighty rushing wind."

By Jesus's time, Jews had come to associate the Pentecost with the giving of the Law at Sinai (e.g., b. Shab. 86b),[11] and thus it is significant that God sent his Spirit to his new community at Pentecost: as the Israelites celebrated Passover and then were given the Law fifty days later, Christ fulfilled the Passover with his death and sent the Spirit fifty days later in order to write God's Law on the hearts of his people. As God formerly had saved Noah and his family from judgment in the ark, commanded Abraham's descendants to be circumcised, and rescued the Israelites through the Red Sea, now Christians are saved from judgment, spiritually circumcised, and rescued from bondage through the waters of baptism (1 Cor 10:1–2; Col 2:11–12; 1 Pet 3:20–21).[12] Indeed, baptism is a form of dying and rising to new life (Rom 6:3–5). Although we are no longer under the law (Rom 6:14–15), nevertheless God has written his law—summarized in the Ten Words—on our hearts (Jer 31:31–34; Heb 8:8–12). As God originally had created the world as a temple, now Christians, both individually and corporately, are God's temple.[13] As previous temples had been built on the plunder of God's enemies, Christ has plundered the house of Satan (Matt 12:29), from which he gives riches to the Church,

11. That is, on the 6th day of Sivan, which they understood to be a Sabbath.

12. As previously noted, the word 'ark' is found in the OT only in Gen 6–8 and Exod 2:3, 5. Moses's personal exodus foreshadows Israel's corporate exodus, thereby implying that his salvation through the water in the ark foreshadows Israel's salvation through the water as they cross on dry ground. This is how Christian baptism can be compared both to Noah's ark and the crossing of the Red Sea.

13. First Cor 3:16–17; 6:19; 2 Cor 6:16; Eph 2:19–22; 1 Pet 2:5.

his temple (Mark 3:27; Eph 4:7–16). This is the eschatological temple that Haggai had prophesied about (Hag 2:7). God now invites us into his rest (Ezek 37:14; Heb 3:7–4:11).

2. Man

Election

Based on the chronological hints provided in Daniel 9, many Jews already were predicting the coming of the Messiah near the turn of the era.[14] Thus, when the fullness of time had come, God sent his Son into the world (Matt 1:1–17; Gal 4:4). Whereas Adam had been created in the image of God, Jesus Christ is the true image of God (2 Cor 4:4; Col 1:15; Heb 1:3). Whereas previous figures such as Adam, Israel, and the king had been called God's son by his grace and choosing, Jesus was God's eternal and natural Son who had come into the world (e.g., Jn 1:1, 14).[15] According to Luke's genealogy, Jesus is the 77th descendant from Adam (Luke 3:23–38), and scholars have suggested that Luke's genealogy can be divided into eleven groups of seven, which would make Jesus the beginning of the twelfth group, which may represent Israel.[16] Ezekiel had prophesied of a ruler who would unite the houses of Judah and Joseph, thereby resolving the ancient rivalry between the tribes of Judah and Ephraim (Ezek 37:22–24), and it is Jesus Christ, the true David, who does this as Israel's true king. He is, after all, a descendant of David, and thus of the house of Judah (Matt 1:1–16). Whereas previous representatives had been shepherds, Jesus is the Good Shepherd (John 10:7–18; Heb 13:20). Jesus is the true prophet (e.g., Acts 3:22–23), true priest (Heb 4:14–15), and true king (Rev 19:11–16). In short, he is the Christ.

14. Wacholder, "Chronomessianism." Many understood this prophecy to coincide with the Jewish Revolt of AD 66–70: Josephus, *War* 6.312–315; Tacitus, *History*, 5.13; Seutonius, *Lives*, Vespasian 4.

15. Along these lines, Moses was a faithful servant, but Jesus was a faithful son (Heb 3:5–6).

16. Marshall, *Commentary on Luke*, 160; DelHousaye, *The Fourfold Gospel*, 176.

Formed outside; 'going forth'

Jesus is the one who 'went forth' from Bethlehem to be Israel's true ruler (Mic 5:2). Although born in Bethlehem, he was initially formed in Egypt and called out to the Promised Land (Matt 2:13–15). Later he lived in Nazareth, which was held in disrepute during his day (John 1:46) and would come up to Jerusalem to finish his work (Luke 9:51).

Mixed multitude

Jesus never had a sinful nature, nor did he ever sin (Heb 4:15). His sinlessness goes infinitely beyond that of Adam's before the fall: Adam's righteousness was incomplete and his will was unformed, whereas Jesus' righteousness was complete and his will was perfectly formed with God's love.

Mountain and garden

Previously God had made covenants with men while they were in gardens on mountains, sometimes with rivers and trees being present. While Jesus had many significant moments with several of these geographical features,[17] they all coalesced on the last day of Jesus' life: he was arrested in the garden of Gethsemane (John 18:1), found guilty in the temple in the mountain-city of Jerusalem (Matt 26:57–68; 27:33), crucified on the tree of his cross (e.g., Acts 5:30; Gal 3:13; 1 Pet 2:24), and pierced in his side, such that the river of blood and water that poured out became the river of life for all mankind (John 19:34). The trees of life and of the knowledge of good and evil find their fulfillment on the tree on which Jesus was crucified: here we have true knowledge and everlasting life (John 3:14–15; 1 Cor 1:23–24). The cross is simultaneously the tree of the knowledge of good and evil in that it brings death to Christ, but it is

17. For example, the mountain was prominent in Jesus' transfiguration, although it does not seem to be the fulfillment of the mountain theme like the crucifixion was. Also, notice that Jesus initiates the disciples' ministry from a mountain (Matt 28:16). For references to an eschatological mountain (Jerusalem), cf. Isa 2:2–4; 4:5–6; 11:9; 25:6–12; Mic 4:1–2; Zech 14:10–11.

also the tree of life in that it brings life to us. It is here, at the Son of Man's moment of humiliation, that he was most exalted and proved to be the fulfiller of the covenant (John 12:23, 32).[18]

Divine blessing and commands

The blessing and commands theme must be looked at from two different perspectives in order to catch the rich irony that Scripture portrays. On the one hand, during Jesus's life and ministry he was seen as receiving God's blessing and as fulling the original creational commands. Thus, Jesus fully pleased the Father, and it is to him that all should listen (Matt 3:17; 17:5). He had been sent into the world to do his Father's will, the essence of which recapitulated all previous commands to be fruitful, multiply, fill the earth, subdue it, and rule over it (Luke 2:49; Jn 6:38). In fact, many messianic texts speak of the Messiah as 'having dominion' over God's enemies,[19] all of which come true in Jesus Christ.[20]

On the other hand, during Jesus' death he was seen as receiving God's curse and the punishment for having broken all the creational commands. Thus, when Jesus revealed his identity to the chief priest and religious leaders as the Son of God, he was accused of blasphemy and sentenced to death (Mark 14:61–65; John 19:7). He was hung on a tree, which is synonymous with being cursed by God (Deut 21:23; Gal 3:13). He fulfilled the experiences mentioned in Psalm 22, the chief of which is abandonment by God (Ps 22:1; cf. Matt 27:46). While the Romans and Jews were the human actors in Jesus's crucifixion, ultimately it was the Father who was wounding him (Isa 53:4–6, 10). In fact, there is a sense in which Jesus became a curse (Gal 3:13) and was made sin (2 Cor 5:21). However, death was swallowed up in victory with the resurrection of Jesus, who was proclaimed to be God's

18. It is interesting to note that the first piece of land that Abraham purchased in Canaan was a field that had trees and a burial cave (Gen 23:17–20). This is reminiscent of the place where Jesus was betrayed, crucified, and buried.

19. Numbers 24:19; Ps 72:8; 110:2; Amos 9:11–12; Zech 9:10.

20. Acts 15:15–18; Rom 15:8–12; 1 Cor 15:25–26.

Son (Rom 1:3–4) and given the name LORD, which is above every other name (Phil 2:9–11).

The Church

As with the previous stage, these themes are passed on to Christians as well. Although Jesus is God's Son *par excellence* (John 1:18; Heb 1:1–2), we have become God's sons and daughters through the grace of adoption (e.g., John 1:12–13; Eph 1:5), we can pray to God as our Father (Matt 6:9), and we can cry out to him as Abba (Rom 8:14–17; Gal 4:4–7). Although we had been far away, we have been brought near to God (Eph 2:11–13). We have taken off the old man and crucified him (Eph 4:22–24; Col 3:9–10) and have come forth (2 Cor 6:17) and been renewed after the likeness of God's Son (Col 3:10). Now there is no holy mountain from which God must be worshipped (John 4:21–24), but rather the whole earth can be considered a holy mountain in Christ (Heb 12:22–24).[21] To the extent that the garden theme represents fellowship with God, Christians are assured of this reality in the present, since even now they have eternal life (e.g., John 3:36; 5:24; 17:3).[22] Christ, through his gospel, puts a river of life in all who believe (John 4:14).[23] Jeremiah's prophesy that Israel one day would 'be fruitful' and 'multiply' comes true in the Church, as does the exhortation for Israel's king to 'rule' over his enemies (Ps 2:8; 72:8; 110:2, 6; Jer 23:3, 5–6). The Great Commission which

21. Nevertheless, it is true that Christians look forward to a new mountain, known as the heavenly Jerusalem and Mount Zion (Gal 4:26; Heb 12:22; Rev 3:12; 21:2, 10). This corresponds to Ezekiel's vision, where the temple is placed on a very high mountain that has a garden and rivers flowing from it (Ezek 40:2; 47:1, 12). See also Ezekiel's famous shepherd parable, in which God promises to bring his people back to "the mountains of Israel" (Ezek 34:13–14).

22. Nevertheless, an eternal paradise still awaits the believer (Luke 23:43; Rev 2:7). Also, as the Proverbs remind us, wisdom is a tree of life (e.g., Prov 3:18).

23. All of this, of course, reaches its climax in the New Jerusalem, where the themes of mountain, garden, temple, and river all converge (Rev 21:1–4; 22:1–2). It is here where God's original plan for Eden will be fully realized, only this time with the additional glory of redemption.

Jesus gives to his disciples is a re-initiation of the original commandments to be fruitful and subdue the earth (Matt 28:19–20; Luke 24:47). God has initiated his new covenant with Christians (Jer 31:31–34; Heb 8:8–12), and we reaffirm our participation in it through the Lord's Supper (Matt 26:27–29; 1 Cor 11:23–26).[24] As God had given the Israelites the lamb to remember their salvation from Egypt, has he given us the true Passover, Jesus Christ, to remind us of our salvation from spiritual bondage (Matt 26:27–28; 1 Cor 5:7). The many passages which speak of the future, Edenic-like blessing of Jerusalem (Isa 51:3; Ezek 35:33–36) are fulfilled, if only in part, in the Church, which spiritually has become the anticipated reality of the heavenly Jerusalem. Our pastors are made shepherds over God's flock (e.g., 1 Pet 5:2), and in Christ we are all made prophets (e.g., 1 Pet 2:9), priests (e.g., 1 Pet 2:9; Heb 13:15), and kings (e.g., 1 Pet 2:9).

3. Fall

Although some of these themes have been introduced above, they will be given a fuller treatment here. Again, the irony of Jesus being treated as a sinner must not be missed.

Not vigilant

Jesus was constantly vigilant and always looking to the Father in the power of the Spirit, from his first temptation in the wilderness at the beginning of his ministry (Matt 4:1–11) to his last temptation in the garden at the end (Matt 26:36–46). The garden of Gethsemane is located on the Mount of Olives, to the east of Jerusalem, and thus it could be seen to coincide with Adam's supposed settlement and final resting place after he was banished from the garden of Eden and traveled east (Gen 3:24).[25] If this is

24. For other important OT texts having to do with the new covenant, cf. Ezek 11:17–20; 16:59–63.

25. As Adam and David were driven eastward after their sin (Gen 3:24; 2 Sam 15:23), so too does Jesus, the last Adam and new David, travel eastward out of Jerusalem before he is punished as a sinner (John 18:1).

so—at a literal or conceptual level—then the place where the first Adam suffered the consequences for his sin of disobedience was the same place where the last Adam suffered the consequences for his righteous act of obedience.

Woman; deception/seduction; usurpation

As was said above, Jesus was always vigilant, and there was never a time when he was not doing his Father's will (John 8:29). Nevertheless, Satan entered his closest circle through Judas, whom he used to betray Jesus (Luke 22:3; John 13:2, 27). Although the religious leaders had attempted many times to trick Jesus with seemingly impossible theological questions (e.g., Matt 22:15–46)—and thus to usurp his authority—, they never succeeded. Now, however, with the help of Judas, they had an opportunity to overcome him (Mark 14:10–11), or so they thought. Although he was, in truth, king of all, he laid down his life (John 10:17–18) and allowed his authority to be usurped, and to be condemned as an insurrectionist (Mark 15:26–27).

Knowledge of sin

Jesus never committed any sin, and indeed Pilate pronounced him innocent of all charges (John 18:38; 19:4, 6), but he was punished as if he were the vilest of sinners (Matt 27:15–23). The Jews imputed to Jesus the sin of blasphemy for revealing his true identity as God's Son (John 19:7). Jesus was aware that he was being treated as if he had sinned (Matt 27:46).

Curse

Jesus was shamefully mocked and beaten (Matt 26:67–68; 27:26), led off to be crucified (Mark 15:20–21), stripped of his clothes (Matt 27:35),[26] and crucified (e.g., Mark 15:22–25). It is no wonder that Jesus himself thought of this as shameful (Heb 12:2). Since

26. Contrariwise, Adam clothed himself to hide his shame (Gen 3:7).

he was hung on a tree (Gal 3:13) outside of Jerusalem (Heb 13:12; cf. Jn 19:20) with two insurrectionists (Matt 27:38), it seemed clear to the bystanders that Jesus had been cursed by God. Jesus's cry of abandonment by God reinforced their thoughts (Matt 27:46). Jesus was crowned with thorns (Matt 27:29), symbolically taking on himself the emblematic curse of Adam for his sin in the garden (Gen 3:18). Whereas the first Adam brought death into the world by eating from a tree in the garden, the last Adam brought life into the world by offering all to eat from his crucified body (1 Cor 11:23–25).

Forgiveness

There was no forgiveness for Jesus: he was punished unto death. The Serpent had bitten the heal of Eve's promised seed, and his poison has dealt the death blow (Gen 3:15). Although Jesus did not need forgiveness, he forgave his enemies on the cross (Luke 23:34).

The great change, of course, came with Jesus's resurrection. Although Satan tried to usurp his authority first by having him sin (e.g., Matt 4:1–11) and later by having him killed, Jesus triumphed over him and all other spiritual powers on the cross (John 12:31; Col 2:15). Jesus, in fact, was the one who ransacked the place of the dead and led captivity away as his captive (Eph 4:8–9).[27] Although he had been bitten on the heal, he crushed the Serpent's head (Gen 3:15). Although he was stripped of his clothing, he now offers us himself as clothing (Rom 13:14; Gal 3:27). All authority has been given to Jesus, and his authority can never be usurped by Satan (Matt 28:18). Although Jesus was cursed by God, it pleased God to punish him (Isa 53:10), since it was his foreordained plan to do so (1 Cor 2:7–8), by which he could reconcile humanity to himself (2 Cor 5:19).

27. In fact, as the early Christian tradition repeatedly points out, if there were any deception going on during the death of Jesus, it was Jesus deceiving Satan and not vice versa.

The Church

As Christians, we are called to imitate Christ in the power of the Spirit to the glory of the Father. We are called to be vigilant and guard ourselves against the subtle encroachments of the devil (e.g., 2 Cor 11:3; Eph 6:18). Although our good conduct will speak of our innocence (1 Pet 2:15), at times we will be treated as if we were the vilest of sinners (e.g., Matt 5:10–12). We, too, may be counted as a curse amongst humanity, but our death is what brings life to others (2 Cor 4:7–12; Col 1:24–29). Since we have been forgiven by God, we too can forgive our enemies, even though they may persecute us unto death (e.g., Acts 7:60). Now forgiveness is preached to all (Luke 24:47).[28]

4. Division

Division[29]

The theme of division between the seed may be looked at from two different perspectives. On the one hand, instead of seeing a division that is provoked by sin, we see a unity that is brought about by Jesus' righteousness. Here Cullmann's principle of progressive advance powerfully comes into view. After Jesus' resurrection, the Apostles and a few close disciples such as Mary and the women who ministered to Jesus can be seen as a kind of renewed remnant. Then, some 120 other Jews were worshipping the Lord together in Jerusalem (Acts 1:12–15), which can be seen as the renewed tribe of Judah. Then, pious Jews from all around the world gathered in Jerusalem for the feast of Pentecost, and some 3,000 repented and

28. The many parallels with the Joseph narrative should not be missed: although innocent, he was tempted by a deceitful woman, removed from his place of authority, and treated as a guilty man. Although he was clothed, he was stripped as he fled. He was thrown in jail—a kind of death and/or burial—with two condemned criminals, one innocent and one guilty. Later he was released—a type of resurrection—and seated at the right hand of Pharaoh.

29. The two thieves on the become paradigmatic of the two seeds that began with Cain and Abel: both are guilty, but one turns to God in repentance and faith, while the other continues to rebel against God until death cross (Luke 23:32, 39–43).

believed and were filled with the Holy Spirit (Acts 2), which can be seen as the renewed twelve tribes. Then, Samaritans were brought into the Church, again receiving the Holy Spirit (Acts 8:4–25), which can be seen as a renewed community that goes beyond pure-bred Jews to embrace Jews of a mixed background. Then, the Ethiopian eunuch was baptized after reading about the suffering Servant in Isaiah 53 (Acts 8:26–38). Although the eunuch's significance is manifold, Luke portrays him as one on the fringes of Judaism: he was not a racial Jew of pure or mixed descent, but he was reading their holy book. Then, Cornelius and his household heard the Gospel from Peter and received the Holy Spirit and were baptized (Acts 10). Cornelius's conversion is significant because he is not a racial or fringe Jew, but rather a pure Gentile, who is nevertheless called a "God-fearer" (Acts 10:2). Finally, Paul's missionary journeys end in the capital of the known world, Rome (Acts 13–28), which essentially means that the Gospel has reached the center of the known world and will go out from there to its furthest limits. The author of Revelation could rightly speak of heaven being filled with people from every tribe, language, people, and nation (Rev 5:9). In fact, the end of the world will not come about until the Gospel has been preached to every nation (Mark 13:10; Matt 24:14). Thus, if we were to complete the chiasm that we began in the introduction, the entire biblical story would look as follows, with Christ functioning as the center of biblical time:[30]

30. I am not arguing that Luke had my scheme in mind, but nevertheless the parallels are astounding. Another way of showing the progressive advance would be the following, suggested to me by Warren Gage: after the Pentecostal reversal of Babel's tower, Luke gives three conversion narratives on "roads" leaving Jerusalem: the Ethiopian (Ham), Paul (Shem), and Cornelius (Japheth). Whatever way one prefers, the point is the same: Luke is showing the steady advance of the Gospel throughout the whole world.

On the other hand, while it is true that Jesus unites all mankind, it is also true that not everyone wishes to repent of their sin and submit to Jesus's reign. To use biblical language, not all the descendants of the first Adam are descendants of the last Adam, but only those who accept the Gospel (Rom 5:12–21). Only those who 'call' on the name of the Lord will be saved (Joel 2:32; Acts 2:21; Rom 10:13). Thus, just as there was a division between the seed of the serpent and the seed of the woman in the garden of Eden (Gen 3:15), there continues to be a division between the spiritual seed of the serpent and the spiritual seed of Jesus (John

8:33, 44), one that is reminiscent of the division between Cain and Abel (1 John 3:8, 11–15).

Persecution

Although God is sovereign over all, nevertheless Satan and his evil host enjoy a certain level of power and authority over this world (Luke 4:6; 2 Cor 4:4; Eph 2:2). They function as the older and more powerful enemies of God who persecute the younger and weaker sons of God. Satan persecuted Jesus while on earth (John 15:20), and he continues to do so by persecuting the Church (Acts 9:4–5).

Cities

Although Satan has sought to establish his own earthly kingdom (Matt 4:8–9), Jesus entrusted himself to his Father and called on him (Matt 4:10; Luke 23:46). The Son of Man did not have so much as a place where he could lay his head (Matt 8:20). Satan will build his Babylon, but ultimately it will be overthrown (Rev 17–18).

Apostasy; inter-marriage

On various occasions, Satan tempted Jesus to sin, such as when he tempted him in the wilderness (Matt 4:1–11) or through Peter's words to abandon the way of the cross (Matt 16:21–23). But although he was tempted in every way as we are, he remained faithful and never sinned (Heb 4:15).

Prophet; preacher of righteousness

Jesus needed no prophet or preacher of righteousness, but he has given to the Church apostles, prophets, evangelists, shepherds, teachers, and all sorts of other gifts to point us back to himself (1 Cor 12; Eph 4:11–14)

Affliction; 'crying out'

Although the Egyptians and Solomon afflicted God's people with burdens, Jesus is the one who bore the burdens of our sins on the cross (Isa 53:4, 11).

The Church

Christians do not seek to establish their own kingdom, but rather to live as pilgrims, call on the Lord, and await the eternal city that God will bring with his kingdom (Heb 11:8–16). Our weapons are not earthly, but rather spiritual (2 Cor 10:3–6; Eph 6:10–18).

As with previous cycles, the major concern for God's people is apostasy (e.g., John 17:15). In fact, Paul draws a direct parallel between the serpent's deception of Eve in the garden and the Church's deception in the present age (2 Cor 11:3). Spiritual inter-marriage with heterodoxy and heteropraxy becomes the chief way by which Christians can become unfaithful to the Lord,[31] although it should be noted that this often can be manifested in physical inter-marriage with non-Christians (cf. 1 Cor 7:39; 2 Cor 6:14), something that must be guarded against.

Similar to how God 'drove' Adam and Eve from the garden and the Israelites 'drove' the Canaanites from the Promised Land, the Church is to expel false Christians from its midst (1 Cor 5:5; cf. 2 Thess 3:6, 14–15; 1 Tim 1:20).

As in previous cycles, the themes of persecution and apostasy reappear: in the vision that John gives in Revelation 13, the beast from the sea makes war with the saints (v. 7) and the beast from the earth deceives those who dwell on the earth (vv. 14–18). In order to keep his people vigilant against apostasy, God has sent prophets/preachers of righteousness to call his people back to the truth. Apostles, prophets, evangelists, pastors, and teachers are the most formal way of doing so (Eph 4:11), but since the whole community is filled with God's Spirit, each of us has the responsibility to exhort one another (e.g., Heb 10:24–25).

31. For example, 2 Cor 11:2; Gal 1:6–9; Phil 3:2; 2 Pet 2:1–3.

What we should be ready for, however, is the certainty of affliction and suffering for righteousness and the name of Jesus (e.g., Matt 5:10–12; 2 Thess 1:2–4; 2 Tim 3:12).[32] We are to wait patiently in our suffering and for the coming of the Lord, who will set all things right (Jas 5:7–12). God's apparent slowness in coming is not intended to discourage us, but rather is a sign of his patience, for he wants all to repent and become his own (2 Pet 3:9). Our crying out to God will not go unheeded (Rev 6:9–10).

5. Judgment

Chaos; flood

One day, the Lord will come and judge all mankind. It is described as "the wrath to come" (1 Thess 1:10). Had the Lord not shortened the days, all would have been swept away in the flood of God's wrath (Mark 13:20). Drawing a parallel with the very first judgment, Jesus said that his coming will be reminiscent of the days of Noah (Matt 24:37–39; 2 Pet 2:5),[33] and Paul said it will be like a thief in the night, when people least expect it (1 Thess 5:2–4).

Deliverance of righteous remnant

Jesus will come to judge the ungodly and save the righteous,[34] at which time he will separate the wheat from the weeds (Matt 13:24–30). Jesus will destroy "the lawless one" (2 Thess 2:8), who can be seen as the incarnation of chaos itself. God will involve Christians in some of the judgment: God will crush Satan under our feet (Rom 16:20), and we will even judge angels (1 Cor 6:3).

32. In an incredible twist of irony, physical Jerusalem—emblematic at a spiritual level of all mankind apart from God—has become spiritual Babylon and Egypt (Rev 11:8), and now persecutes those of heavenly Jerusalem (Gal 4:24–31; 1 Thess 2:15).

33. Another significant parallel is that of Sodom (Luke 17:28–29; 2 Pet 2:6–8). As rain brought Noah's flood (Gen 7:4), so too did "rain" overthrow Sodom (Gen 19:24). For further parallels, cf. Gage, *Gospel of Genesis*, 63–64.

34. Matthew 24:30–31; 2 Thess 1:5–12; 2 Pet 3:7–9, 12–13.

6. Eternity

The final judgment provides the background in which God establishes his eternal kingdom. The prophets prophesied of the eschatological garden-like state of the land of Israel (and beyond).[35] The removal of the sea (Rev 21:1) speaks to the removal of the waters of chaos and judgment of mankind, as well as of the removal of sea monsters. There will be no temple, for God and the Lamb will be its temple (Rev 21:22). There will be no need of the sun and moon, because God and the Lamb will be its light (Rev 21:23), and there will be no more dark night (Rev 22:5). The river of life will be there, flowing from God and the Lamb (Rev 22:1). The tree of life will be there, growing along the banks of the river of life (Rev 22:2; cf. 2:7). Thus, humanity will finally fulfill God's original purpose: to dwell with God in the garden-temple of the holy city of Edenic Jerusalem.

35. Isaiah 30:23–26; 35:5–10; 41:17–20; 51:3 (Eden and garden); 58:11; Jer 31:12 (garden).

Appendix I: Key Hebrew Vocabulary

THIS LIST IS ARRANGED in alphabetical order following the English alphabet and is based on simple glosses provided for each Hebrew word. For each word, after the English gloss comes the Hebrew word itself, followed by a transliteration to aid in pronunciation. Some of these words are taken up into the New Testament, but since New Testament Greek does not provide a one-for-one translation of these Old Testament Hebrew words, I have not included any Greek vocabulary here.

1. Altar: מִזְבֵּחַ (mizbeah)
2. Ark: תֵּבָה (tevah)
3. Be fruitful: פרה (parah)
4. Be strong: עצם (ʿatsam)
5. Blameless: תָּמִים (tamim)
6. Bless: ברך (barak)
7. Break faith: מעל (maʿal)
8. Burnt offering: עוֹלָה (ʿolah)
9. Call: see name
10. Cherub: כְּרוּב (cherub)

11. Clean: טָהוֹר (tahor)
12. Clever, cunning: עָרוּם and עָרְמָה (ʿarum and ʿarmah)
13. Clothe: לבשׁ (lavash)
14. Cool of the day: רוּחַ הַיּוֹם (ruah hayyom)
15. Come down: ירד (yarad)
16. Come out: see go forth
17. Corrupt: see destroy
18. Create: ברא (bara')
19. Curse: אָרוּר ('arur)
20. Cry out: צעק and זעק (tsaʿaq and zaʿaq)
21. Cunning: see clever
22. Deep: תְּהוֹם (tehom)
23. Desire: חמד (hamad)
24. Destroy, corrupt: שׁחת (shahath)
25. Drive: גרשׁ (garash)
26. Evil: רָע (raʿ)
27. Fill: מלא (mala')
28. Form: יצר (yatsar)
29. Formless, wasteland: תֹּהוּ (tohu)
30. Gird and girdle: חגר and חֲגֹרָה (hagar and hagorah)
31. Give birth: ילד (yalad)
32. Go forth: יצא (yatsa')
33. Gold: זָהָב (zahab)
34. Good: טוֹב (tob)
35. Guard: see keep
36. Have dominion: רדה (radah)
37. Helper: עֵזֶר (ʿezer)
38. Hover: רחף (rahaph)

39. Image: צֶלֶם (tselem)

40. Keep, guard: שׁמר (shamar)

41. Know: ידע (yada‘)

42. Light: מָאוֹר (ma’or)

43. Likeness: דְּמוּת (demuth)

44. Make wise: שׂכל (sacal)

45. Mixed: עֶרֶב (’ereb)

46. Multiply: רבה (rabah)

47. Name, call: קרא (qara’)

48. Nakedness: עֶרְוָה and עֵירֹם (‘erwah and ‘iram)

49. Nation: גּוֹיִם (goyyim)

50. Onyx stone: אֶבֶן הַשֹּׁהַם (eben hashoham)

51. Plague: מַגֵּפָה (maggephah)

52. Pleasant: תַּאֲוָה (ta’awah)

53. Remember: זכר (zacar)

54. Rest: נוח and שׁבת (noah and shabat)

55. Righteous: צַדִּיק (tsadiq)

56. Scatter: פוץ (puts)

57. Sea: יָם (yam)

58. Sea monster: see serpent

59. See: ראה (ra’ah)

60. Send: שׁלח (shalah)

61. Separate: פרד (parad)

62. Serpent, sea monster: תַּנִּין (tannin)

63. Smell: רוח (ruah)

64. Soothing aroma: רֵיחַ הַנִּיחֹחַ (reah hanihoah)

65. Spirit, wind: רוּחַ (ruah)

66. Subdue: כבשׁ (cabash)

67. Swarm: שׁרץ (sharats)
68. Take: לקח (laqah)
69. Uncover: גלה (galah)
70. Void: בֹּהוּ (bohu)
71. Walk: הלךְ (halak)
72. Wasteland: see formless
73. Wind: see Spirit
74. Wonders: פלא (pala')
75. Work: עבד ('abad)

Appendix II: Implications for Other Disciplines

The reading of the Old Testament and its fulfillment in Jesus Christ presented throughout this book has implications for other disciplines. While this is not the main purpose of this study, I would like to suggest some ways that this reading of Scripture helps us understand other topics and fields of research.

1. The "Six Ages" of History

Beginning with Augustine and becoming very influential thereafter, many ancient theologians understood biblical (and world) history to be divided into six ages: 1) from Adam to Noah; 2) from Noah to Abraham; 3) from Abraham to David; 4) from David to the Babylonian captivity; 5) from the Babylonian captivity to Jesus Christ; 6) from Jesus Christ to the present (presumably continuing until Jesus' second coming).[1]

However, there are two weaknesses with this view. First, these six ages were merely asserted rather than provided with strong exegetical backing. Second, and more importantly, these six ages did

1. Augustine, *On the Catechizing of the Uninstructed*, §22. Graeme Dunphy cites dozens of authors through the fifteenth century who either followed Augustine's scheme or at least had a strong awareness of it; cf. Dunphy, "Six Ages."

not coincide with the three[2] important theological dispensations that were equally accepted by many in antiquity: *ante legem* ("before the Law"), *sub lege* ("under the Law"), and *sub gratia* ("under grace"). The problem was that the third age (from Abraham to David) spanned both *ante legem* and *sub lege*. The table below shows the discrepancy between these two systems:[3]

<table>
<tr><th>Theological dispensation</th><th>Six ages</th></tr>
<tr><td rowspan="3">Ante legem</td><td>Adam</td></tr>
<tr><td>Noah</td></tr>
<tr><td rowspan="2">Abraham</td></tr>
<tr><td rowspan="3">Sub lege</td></tr>
<tr><td>David</td></tr>
<tr><td>Babylonian captivity</td></tr>
<tr><td>Sub gratia</td><td>Jesus</td></tr>
</table>

However, according to the reading of the biblical story presented throughout this book, these two deficiencies have been addressed: the combination and extension of Cullmann's and Gage's insights provide exegetical backing to read Scripture in a way very similar to the one proposed by Augustine, and the insertion of the Moses/Joshua cycle has made it possible to reconcile the biblical ages/cycles with the theological dispensations. Modifying the previous chart in light of our findings, the two systems now can be harmonized in a satisfying way:

2. To be more precise, in his work *Expositio quarundam propositionum ex Epistola apostoli ad Romanos*, Augustine stated that there were four "states": *ante legem*, *sub lege*, *sub gratia*, and *in pace*, but the last is only attainable in eternity (although we inhabit it now through hope).

3. Taken and adapted from Dunphy, "Six Ages," 1370.

Theological dispensation	Six ages
Ante legem	Adam
	Noah
	Abraham
Sub lege	Moses and Joshua
	David
	Babylonian captivity
Sub gratia	Jesus

What we end up with, therefore, is a modern justification for an old Augustinian interpretation of the biblical story that is exegetically sound, more consistent theologically, and with a deeper appreciation of the reason why the cycles exist and how they are driving toward fulfillment in Jesus Christ.

2. Old Testament Methodology

For this and the following two sections, I would like to interact with some of the issues set forth in Gerhard Hasel's classic work on Old Testament theology. To begin, the question of methodology has been an issue that has been highly problematic for Old Testament theologians for the simple reason that imposed schemes do not allow the text to speak for itself, while more text-based schemes do not allow for easy systematization. Hasel identified ten different methodologies, with all of them falling into one of these two errors.[4]

One of the methodologies that he identified and dismissed as having been imposed for dogmatic reasons is called the "Dogmatic–Didactic Method." According to Hasel, this is the "traditional method" of organizing Old Testament theology and follows the tripartite structure of God–Man–Salvation, or, to use the categories of systematic theology, Theology–Anthropology–Soteriology.

4. *Old Testament Theology*, 28–114.

His critique of this method lies in the fact that it is of a "deductive nature" and thus the "OT cannot speak for itself." He astutely asks, "Does the dogmatic approach not ultimately present a theology rooted in the OT rather than the OT's own theology?"[5]

However, based on our findings throughout this work, it can be argued that a version of the "Dogmatic–Didactic Method" is how the Old Testament presents itself to be read. This was pointed out by Warren Gage when he observed that the Genesis 1–7 cycle follows the basic structure of God–Man–Sin–Redemption–Judgment. Of this order he writes, "These categories . . . suggest a bridge from biblical to systematic theology. Cf. the doctrines of theology proper, anthropology, hamartiology, ecclesiology, and eschatology."[6] While Gage applied his cycle broadly to the Old Testament story, our findings suggest that this basic five-point cycle is how the Old Testament presents itself to be interpreted, or at least one way to be interpreted without imposing a foreign paradigm. Each cycle offers new insights into how each doctrine is to be understood and interpreted, and their combined testimony is what allows us to construct an Old Testament theology.

3. The *Mitte* of Old Testament Theology

Another difficult issue facing Old Testament theology is the problem of finding the *Mitte* ("center"). Hasel's survey of the various solutions demonstrates the uncertainty of Old Testament theologians, with some arguing for one center, others for multiple, and others arguing against the idea of a center altogether.[7]

5. *Old Testament Theology*, 39–42. H. G. M. Williamson shares the same hesitation: "For many years now there has been a long-running debate about how best to organize and arrange a 'Theology of the Old Testament.' . . . Traditionally, the major headings of Christian systematic theology have been used: God, creation, man, sin, salvation, life as the people of God, and eschatology. It is self-evident, however, that the Old Testament itself is not arranged according to these categories" (*Ezra and Nehemiah*, 77).

6. *Gospel of Genesis*, 5 (esp. n. 8); cf. 9.

7. *Old Testament Theology*, 139–71. Hasel himself prefers no center (*Old Testament Theology*, 168).

What our findings demonstrate is that the *Mitte* of Old Testament theology is the five-stage cycle that is driving itself towards fulfillment in Jesus Christ, and that many other previously offered solutions find their home within these categories. For example, those who argue for covenant, election, and/or communion as the center of Old Testament theology are really addressing the "Man" stage of the cycle and its subsequent development, and those who argue for God as warrior as the center are really addressing the "Judgment" and/or "Creation" stages.

4. The Relationship Between the Old and New Testaments

Hasel also addresses the issue of the relationship between the two Testaments, and the difficulties involved in connecting Old Testament theology with the New Testament.[8] What we have seen, however, is that Cullmann's thesis of progressive reduction is a solution to this dilemma. According to our findings, the Old Testament repeatedly and systematically demonstrates that mankind is represented by a progressively smaller group of people, and that the story ends with the failure of the remnant. The Old Testament ends, therefore, with mankind's failure to represent God to the world. Yet the reader also knows that God has spoken his word of promise to save his people. Here we have a tremendous tension: What will have the final word: mankind's failure or God's promise?

The Old Testament's harmony has been left unresolved, and it is begging for someone to play the final note, which will bring resolution and fulfillment to the entire score. And it is this uneasiness that justifies us to move organically from the Old Testament to the New. Jesus Christ is the new Adam, the new Noah, the true seed of Abraham, the better Moses, the true Joshua, the better David, and the only faithful remnant, and it is upon him that all of humanity's hope rest.

8. *Old Testament Theology*, 172–93.

5. Other World Religions

Finally, if the basic argument presented throughout this book is correct, then Christianity is the definitive fulfillment of the Jewish Scriptures, with no conceivable subsequent fulfillment. Here, I will limit my comments to those religions who take the Jewish Scriptures to be authoritative.

Regarding Judaism, the power of the book's argument is that the Old Testament itself is driving toward a resolution that can only be fulfilled in someone who comes around the time of Christ. That this was understood to be the case is confirmed by the fact that, shortly before and after Jesus' coming, there was a greater cluster of messianic claimants than any other time in history. The Jews themselves were sensing that fulfillment was near, which is what Christians claim as well, the only difference being that Christians see the fulfillment happening in Christ, whereas Jews hoped it would have happened in Simon Bar Kokhba.

Regarding other religions such as Islam and Mormonism—who argue, in their own ways, that further revelation is needed after Christ—, it must be restated that Christ is the center of redemption history, and thus it would be incoherent to posit the need for further revelation after him. The very idea of a chiasm, shaped like an X, makes it incoherent to suggest that the center point was not truly the center, but rather penultimate. Anyone who accepts the funnel-like shape of the Old Testament narrative that has been argued for throughout this book should recognize the unique role that Christ plays in the progression of this narrative, and this role cannot be superseded by any further revelation.

Appendix III: Potential and Partial Cycles

Some who read the biblical story according to the scheme that has been presented throughout this book may argue that other cycles ought to have been inserted at various points in the narrative. This should not be surprising, since Scripture often reuses previous characters and events to portray contemporary ones. Thus, many figures are recast as a new Moses, many sins as an Edenic fall, many judgments as a flood, etc.

Readers should know why these potential and partial cycles were not included in my main argument. First, the number seven seemed like a fitting number of cycles to include in the Old Testament, with Jesus functioning as something similar to early Christian "eighth day" theology. A full week, as it were, of cycles had to run their course to prepare God's people for the fulfillment of all, Christ himself, who initiates a kind of "new day" with his coming. Second, many of these cycles did not contain all the stages necessary to make a complete cycle. Parts were present, for sure, but not all five, from beginning to end (e.g., Samuel and Saul). Finally, some potential cycles did not continue to advance the biblical story as it was progressing through God's chosen line. Perhaps there was a noticeable cycle (e.g., Solomon), but it seemed to me to advance a minor plot or character as opposed to the overarching narrative of the biblical story.

Nevertheless, for those interested readers, and with the hopes that others might be able to come to deeper insights than I have, I have included that potential and partial cycles that I did not include in the main argument of the book. In some cases, the information included here was used previously in the main argument of the book.

Samuel and Saul[1]

1. Creation

Creation from chaos

As the period of the Judges ends, Israel finds itself with a corrupt leadership and priesthood (e.g., Judg 17–18). By the opening of 1 Samuel, the priesthood had been severely compromised (1 Sam 2:12–17, 22–25), the word of the LORD was rare (1 Sam 3:1), and God had chosen to reveal himself, not to a Levitical priest or well-known prophet, but to an Ephraimite boy, Samuel (1 Sam 3:1–4:1). Eli's lack of insight and vision (1 Sam 1:12–13; 3:2; 4:15) combined with his greed and obesity (1 Sam 2:29, 32; 4:18) are reminiscent of Isaac's conditions —physical and spiritual— in his old age, after he had stopped being vigilant and failed to trust in the LORD. Additionally, the LORD had closed Hannah's womb, causing great suffering (1 Sam 1:6–7, 10, 16).

Nevertheless, in the midst of this darkness, God began to create again. Hannah was able to see the beginning of God's creation and deliverance, which she voiced in her prayer in a series of contrasts: the mighty are broken, but the feeble become strong; the full are hungry, but the hungry are full; the barren woman has children, but the mother is forlorn; the rich are poor, but the poor are rich; God's enemies will be destroyed, but the faithful will be kept safe (1 Sam 2:1–10). In addition, she used creation language

1. Cf. Roberts and Wilson, *Echoes of Exodus*, 88–92. Also, cf. chapter 6 above.

when she spoke of the pillars of the earth belonging to the LORD, on which he had set the world (1 Sam 2:8).

Creation battle

In the opening chapters of 1 Samuel, God destroys three foes at once: the corrupt priests, the corrupt judge, and the Philistines. The corrupt priests Hophni and Phineas were killed in battle (1 Sam 4:11), and the corrupt judge Eli was killed upon hearing the report of Israel's defeat in battle (1 Sam 4:18). This was part of God's judgment on the house of Eli (1 Sam 2:27–36; 3:11–14).

The recounting of the defeat of the Philistines is more extended. As 1 Samuel 4 recounts a type of exile for Israel as it loses the ark of the covenant to the Philistines, 1 Samuel 5 begins the story of a new creation, especially as it centers on the destiny of the ark of the LORD. The ark's experiences are filtered through various Exodus motifs. None of this was to any avail, however, and the Israelites eventually freed themselves from Philistine bondage, thanks to the intervention of the LORD (1 Sam 7:10–11, 13–14; 9:16).

God's Spirit

God's personal presence was with Samuel, which implies his Spirit (1 Sam 3:2–14, 21).

God's word

Although God's word was rare in those days (1 Sam 3:1), he began to speak again, this time to Samuel (1 Sam 3:2–14, 21).

Temple

Although God had rejected Shiloh (Ps 78:60) and the ark had stayed in Kiriath-jearim for some twenty years (1 Sam 7:1–2), Samuel continued to build altars in places like the Ephraimite town of Ramah (1 Sam 7:17; cf. 9:10–14).

Rest

The LORD miraculously and decisively delivered Israel from the Philistines under Samuel's leadership (1 Sam 7:5–14), and Saul fought against Israel's surrounding neighbors —Moab, Ammon, Edom, Zobah, Philistine, and Amalek— and had victory on every side (1 Sam 14:47–48). Israel's borders are once again secure, and she is given rest.

2. Man

Election.

Similar to how God had worked through Moses and Aaron in the previous cycle, he does so again through Samuel and Saul. Samuel was born thanks to a vow that Hannah had made to the LORD, and she promised that he would lead a Nazarite-like life (1 Sam 1:11). Although the LORD had closed her womb, he now opens it (1 Sam 1:19–20). Samuel is lent to the LORD for his entire life and he continues to minister before the LORD and to grow in favor with the LORD and with man (1 Sam 1:28; 2:18, 21, 26). All Israel recognizes that he is the LORD's prophet (1 Sam 3:20), and all that he says comes true (1 Sam 9:6). As with those before him, he functions as prophet (1 Sam 3:20), priest (e.g., 1 Sam 2:25), and king (1 Sam 7:15–17).

Saul was a Benjaminite, who was tall and handsome (1 Sam 9:1–2; 10:23–24). God had chosen him to be a prince and king over the Israelites (1 Sam 9:15–17). Saul prophesies (1 Sam 10:10–13) and rules over Israel (1 Sam 10:17–27), but when he attempts to fulfill the role of priest, he fails miserably (1 Sam 13:8–14).

Formed outside; 'go forth'

Samuel was born and weaned in Ramah, but later taken to Shiloh where the tabernacle was located (1 Sam 1:21–28; 2:11). When Hannah shared her prayer request with Eli, he told her to 'go forth' in peace (1 Sam 1:17). Israel 'went forth' to renew the kingdom at Gilgal (1 Sam 11:14–15).

Mixed multitude

Samuel's sons did not walk in the ways of his father, but rather turned after bribes (1 Sam 8:1–2). Similarly, Saul's heart was never formed to follow God. He came from the tribe of Benjamin, which the book of Judges shows to be one of the most morally corrupt of all the tribes of Israel (Judg 19–21).

Mountain and garden

There does not appear to be any discernable emphasis on a mountain or garden in this cycle.

Divine blessing and commands

The fact that Saul was anointed king over Israel implies that he was blessed by God and the inheritor of the divine blessing and commands. His war with his surrounding neighbors —Moab, Ammon, Edom, Zobah, Philistine, and Amalek— shows his intent to subdue the land (1 Sam 14:47–18).

3. Fall

Although initially Saul had demonstrated a certain amount of humility and obedience (1 Sam 11) and was given a certain amount of success early in his reign (1 Sam 14:47–48), this quickly stopped and his foolish and sinful actions led to him being rejected by God (1 Sam 13–15). Very telling of Saul's true character is the fact that although he had been rejected by God, he only seemed to care about his earthly kingdom (1 Sam 15:24–31). Thus, he was more concerned with calling a kingdom after his own name rather than calling on the name of the Lord in repentance and faith.

Not vigilant

Saul's foolish and sinful nature begin to show in his unlawful sacrifice at Gilgal and the rash vow that he made during his attack on the Philistines (1 Sam 13:8–14; 14:24–45). The key moment came when he disobeyed God's command to annihilate the Amalekites: instead of destroying them as God had commanded, he spared king Agag and the best of the cattle (1 Sam 15:9).

Woman; deception/seduction; usurpation

Saul was not willing to destroy the best of the plunder, including king Agag (1 Sam 15:9). By sparing them, he had usurped his own right to rule over Israel and been dethroned *de jure* if not yet *de facto* (1 Sam 15:22–23).

Knowledge of sin

After being rebuked by Samuel, Saul confessed his sin (1 Sam 15:24, 30). Instead of tearing his clothes in repentance, he tore Samuel's robe in an attempt to spare his reputation (1 Sam 15:27). Saul's repentance is merely external and has nothing to do with true repentance and faith.

Curse

Samuel told Saul that the kingdom had been taken away from him and given to another (1 Sam 15:22–28).

Forgiveness

Saul appears to have been forgiven, or at least save face, as Samuel returned with Saul and worshipped the LORD (1 Sam 15:31).

4. Division

Division

Early in Saul's reign, he loved David and considered him a great asset (1 Sam 16:21). Shortly thereafter, however, he turned against David and forced him into exile (e.g., 1 Sam 18:9). Saul was older and had more political and military power than David, while David was still a young man and relied primarily on a few outcasts for support (1 Sam 22:1–2). This dynamic foreshadows the future division between the northern and southern kingdoms, respectively.

Persecution.

Saul attempted to kill David on several occasions (e.g., 1 Sam 18:10–11) and even goes so far as massacring innocent priests who unknowingly helped David during one of his flights (1 Sam 22:6–19). This is a clear example of the older, stronger, and ungodly persecuting the younger, weaker, and godly.

5. Judgment

This is where the cycle appears to stop, thus making it incomplete.

Solomon

This is the most complete cycle that was not included in the primary text of the book. Aside from a few themes, a near-complete cycle can be reproduced. The reason why it was not included is because it impinged on the David cycle and there was no clear emphasis on the covenant. Of all the cycles presented here, this is probably the best candidate to be recognized as a full cycle, which would necessitate recalibrating chapter 7 above.

1. Creation

Creation from chaos

In the opening chapters of 1 Kings, King David dies, Adonijah usurps the throne of Israel, and Joab and Abiathar the priest have joined in the ceremonies. The old king is dead, and a usurper is attempting to claim the throne. This is the recipe for chaos.[2]

2. As Burke Long writes, "In seeing 1 Kings 1 as a part of this storied world of human and human-divine relationships, we finally have come to the heart of the story's power. It is the Genesis myth in another dress: cosmos --> chaos --> cosmos" ("A Darkness between Brothers," 89).

Creation battle[3]

Solomon eliminates three main opponents: Joab (military leader), Shimei (royal descendant and adversary), and Adonijah (throne contender) aided by Nathan (prophet).[4]

God's word

With the establishment of the temple in Jerusalem and the placement of the ark in the Most Holy Place, the Ten Words that God had given Moses at Horeb have arrived in Jerusalem (1 Kgs 8:9). The societal order that God has established through the reigns of David and Solomon are completed and perfected by the moral order represented in the Ten Words.

Temple

With the arrival of Solomon to the throne, the original plan from the time of the Exodus has been fulfilled: God has chosen his mountain and established his temple where his people can worship him (Deut 12:5–14).[5] As with creation and the tabernacle

3. After speaking of the pattern of the contrast between death and life Pharaoh and Moses, Eli and Samuel, and Samuel's sons and kingship in Israel, Burke Long writes, "So it is entirely right and conventional that the story of Solomon's rise should begin with an intimation of decay and dissonance, as if the old must give way to the new, but not without struggle and death" ("A Darkness between Brothers," 84). Adonijah has a legitimate claim to the throne: in addition to being favored by David and next in line now that Absalom is dead, he is "aggressive, self-assured, handsome, powerful, successfully gathering his supporters and acting the kingly office" (Long, "A Darkness between Brothers," 86). Thus, as Isaac had preferred Esau over Jacob, it seems that David prefers Adonijah over Solomon.

4. God will raise three enemies to plague Solomon, all mentioned in 1 Kgs 11: Hadad the Edomite (military leader, royal descent), Rezon (royal descendant and adversary), and Jeroboam (throne contender), aided by Ahijah (prophet). For this connection, cf. Parker, "Repetition as a Structure Device," 21–22).

5. Moses' earlier prophecy of "the place, O Lord, which you have made for your abode" (Exod 15:17) is fulfilled in Solomon's temple (1 Kgs 8:13; cf. 2 Chr 6:2).

before, the temple is built from plunder taken from Israel's enemies (1 Chr 26:27). As the glory of the LORD, manifested as a cloud, had filled the tabernacle that Moses had made, now again his glory fills the temple that David and Solomon had made (1 Kgs 8:10–11).[6] King Solomon decorated the temple with flowers (lilies), fruits (pomegranates), and trees (palm trees), probably to resemble the garden of Eden. Also it is possible that living trees (esp. olive) were growing in the temple courts, which would be an even stronger link with the garden.[7] Whereas Babel had been built for the name of its builders, the Jerusalem temple was built for the name of the LORD (1 Kgs 8:20). In this sense, Mount Zion functions as a kind of anti-Tower of Babel.

Rest

As God had given 'rest' to Adam in the garden, he gives 'rest' to Solomon and the whole of Israel (1 Kgs 5:4; 8:56). Indeed, Solomon's initial reign was a time of 'peace' (1 Kgs 4:26 [MT: 5:4]). Although David was a man of bloodshed, Solomon is a son of 'rest' (1 Chr 22:6–10, 17–19; cf. 28:3).

2. Man[8]

Election

Similar to Adam and Eve, who were so naïve that they are described in child-like terms in the garden and lacked certain

6. Solomon built the temple that his father had planned (1 Kgs 5:1–6:38; 7:13–8:11; 2 Chr 2:1–5:1).

7. Genesis 2:9; 1 Kgs 6:18, 29; 7:18–26, 49; Ps 52:8; 92:12. Marvin Tate writes: "There is little reason to doubt (as some do) that olive trees actually grew in the area of the temple on Mount Zion. Cypress and olive trees grow in the Dome of the Rock area of Jerusalem today. Trees were common in temple areas throughout the ancient Near East, symbols of life, fertility, and power" (*Psalms 51–100*, 38). Othmar Keel similarly argues that the temple trees were living reminders of God's invisible, mysterious blessing which was operative in them and in his people (*Symbolism*, 135–36, 354).

8. John Davies writes: "A fruitful way of doing justice to the complex data the book of Kings provides on Solomon is to see him as an Adam figure who

knowledge (e.g., Gen 2:28; 3:5), Solomon is portrayed as a "little child" who lacks knowledge (1 Kgs 3:7). God gave Solomon "a wise and discerning mind" beyond all others (1 Kgs 3:12).[9] Solomon asks to discern between 'good' and 'evil,' almost as if not wanting to commit the same folly as Adam and Eve (1 Kgs 3:9).

Mountain and garden

Solomon was acclaimed king at Gihon, a river at Jerusalem that carries the same name as one of the four rivers in Eden (1 Kgs 1:33, 38, 45). Just before dying, David charges him to 'keep' God's laws, thus evoking Adam's call to 'keep' the garden and the priestly duty to 'keep' the tabernacle/temple (1 Kgs 2:2–3). He had mastery knowledge of flora and fauna (1 Kgs 4:33 [MT: 5:13]), and his triennial shipments included animals that would inhabit a royal garden (1 Kgs 10:22), all of which evoke the idea of Solomon in a garden-like atmosphere.

Solomon builds the first temple at an even higher point on the mountain than where his father had set up the ark of the covenant (e.g., 2 Sam 24:18–20), thereby evoking once again the man–mountain–garden complex (1 Kgs 8:1–4; 2 Chr 3:1).[10] Adding to the garden theme, some texts refer to the Israelite people with garden imagery, especially in connection with their presence in the temple (2 Sam 7:10; Ps 52:8; 80:8–11; 92:12–14). Psalm 46 is interesting for at least two reasons. First, in verse 4, it

---

on the one hand typifies a fulfillment of aspirations for a restored Eden, while on the other hand being responsible, through his disobedience, for a second expulsion from the sanctuary-land and the end of the monarchy—that is, the loss of Yahweh's visible rule and protection, and of Israel's dignity among the nations. Through such a portrayal, the writer keeps alive the prospect of a new Adam in a new creation beyond the covenant failure presided over by Solomon" ("'Discerning Between Good and Evil,'" 40).

9. "We perceive Solomon as the nearest we come to an ideal ruler and mediator conceived in human terms. Solomon's greatness, and that of his kingdom, outstrips that of his illustrious father in many respects" (Davies, "'Discerning Between Good and Evil,'" 56).

10. According to Ezekiel, the eschatological temple will also be on a mountain, with lush vegetation, and with rivers flowing forth from it (Ezek 47:1, 12).

associates a river with Jerusalem. Second, in verses 1–7 the chaos theme is brought into light: even though chaos comes back into the world (vv. 1–3), God's people can trust in him, because he dwells in Jerusalem (vv. 4–7). Solomon embellished the temple and its furnishings with even more garden-like imagery: 1 Kings 6–7 mentions lilies, garlands, flowers, palm trees, lions, oxen, and cherubs as decorations.

Divine blessing and commands

God blessed Solomon: under him, the people became so great that they could not be numbered, thus evoking both the original creation mandate and the promise given to Abraham (1 Kgs 3:8). He 'had dominion' from the Euphrates to Egypt (1 Kgs 4:24 [MT: 5:1]).[11] Solomon was 'blessed' by God and the people (1 Kgs 2:45; 8:66). As Joshua had claimed that "not one word had failed" of all the promises that God had made to the patriarchs (Jos 23:14), Solomon claims that "not one word has failed" of all the promises that God had made through Moses (1 Kgs 8:55–56).[12] As the serpent and its cursed seed was to lick the dust (Gen 3:14), so too is Israel's king's enemies are to lick the dust (Ps 72:9). As with many before him, Solomon was portrayed as a prophet (1 Kgs 3:5; 6:11; 9:2;[13] cf. *Ps. Sol.* 2:24–35), priest (1 Kgs 3:3–4; 8:5, 14, 64), and king (e.g., 1 Kgs 1:34).

3. Fall

Not vigilant

Already before his coronation, the author of the book of Kings had hinted that he (and his mother, Bathsheba) would be sinners (1

11. Also to be noticed is the reference to the Euphrates, making yet another connection with the creation account (Gen 2:14).

12. The Hebrew expression is the same in both texts.

13. The language of the LORD "appearing" (Heb: ראה) to someone is used in Gen 12:7 with reference to Abraham, who was, indeed, called a prophet (Gen 20:7).

Kgs 1:21). Whereas God's first appearance to Solomon was filled with hope and promise (1 Kgs 3:1–15), his second appearance was more negative and prophetically warns Solomon of the dangers of falling away (1 Kgs 9:1–10).[14] While it is true that Solomon's downfall is not mentioned until 1 Kings 11:1, on numerous previous occasions the author reminds us that Solomon had taken an Egyptian wife (1 Kgs 3:1; 7:8; 9:16, 24). This repeated connection between Solomon and Egypt is not arbitrary, as the author is implying that Solomon was slowly taking the country back to Egyptian slavery: the hard service and heavy yoke he placed on his people evokes the Egyptians' treatment of the Israelites during their slavery (1 Kgs 12:4; cf. Exod 1:14; 6:9; Lev 26:13), his use of forced labor evokes the tower of Babel and Egypt (1 Kgs 4:6; 11:28; 12:18), and his building of store cities evokes the Egyptian store cities Pithom and Rameses (1 Kgs 9:19; cf. Exod 1:11).

Despite what is written about the expected conduct of a king in Deuteronomy 17:14–17, Solomon broke almost the whole standard of conduct mentioned therein: he let a foreigner rule over some of his subjects (1 Kgs 9:11), acquired horses for himself (1 Kgs 10:26–29), acquired many wives for himself (1 Kgs 11:3), and acquired excessive silver and gold for himself (1 Kgs 10:14–15, 27). Although he had prayed to discern between good and evil (1 Kgs 3:9), he failed like Adam and Eve.

Woman; deception/seduction; usurpation

As Adam fell by listening to his wife (Gen 3:17), Solomon fell by letting his wives turn away his heart (1 Kgs 11:3; cf. Neh 13:26). Whereas earlier Solomon had built a temple for God (1 Kgs 6–8), later he builds high places for foreign gods (1 Kgs 11:7–8).[15] Whereas earlier Solomon had used his wisdom to bring justice to

14. "Thus, the first dream depicts the relative peace that will characterize the first section of the narrative (chapters 3–8) whereas the second dream anticipates the demise of the kingdom, characteristic of the second section of the narrative (9.1–11.14)" (Parker, "Repetition as a Structure Device," 22).

15. In fact, according to 2 Kgs 23:13, Solomon built his abominations on the Olivet Ridge east of Zion, which was topographically higher than Zion.

his people (1 Kgs 3:16–28), now he uses it to amass wealth and power for himself (e.g., 1 Kgs 10:14–29).

Knowledge of sin

Similar to how Adam had been made aware of the irreversible consequences of his sin and tried to conceal the consequences, Solomon is made known of the division of his kingdom and seeks to kill Jeroboam, the future king of the northern tribes, because of his apostasy (1 Kgs 11:9–13, 40).

Curse

As God had rebuked Adam for his sin, Solomon was cursed by knowing that the kingdom would be torn away from him and given to his servant (1 Kgs 11:11), something which Ecclesiastes mourns (Eccl 2:18–21; 6:1–2).

Forgiveness

God did not tear the whole kingdom away from Solomon during his own life, but rather waited until his son was on the throne and spared him one tribe (1 Kgs 11:12–13).

4. Division

Division

Solomon's united rule over the twelve tribes of Israel hardly outlives his own reign, with signs of weakness and the prophesy of division taking place during Solomon's reign (1 Kgs 11). The kingdom splits into two shortly after Solomon's death.

King Jeroboam began his reign by essentially reenacting the golden calf episode of Exodus 32: he made golden calves, declared that they were the ones who brought Israel out of Egypt, and observed a festival (1 Kgs 12:28–33; cf. Exod 32:4–6). The biblical verdict for both stories was the same: it was a great sin (2 Kgs 17:21; cf. Exod 32:21, 30–31). Jeroboam even named his sons Nadab and Abijah, eerily reminiscent of the sons of Aaron who rebelled against Moses and were consumed by fire from the LORD (1 Kgs 14:1, 20; cf. Lev 10:1–2).[16]

Persecution

The northern and southern kingdoms, the former of which was clearly the more dominant with regard to land and population, lived in near-perpetual conflict, often with the northern kingdom exercising direct or indirect authority over the southern (e.g., 1 Kgs 11:39).

Cities

Under the leadership of king Jeroboam, the cities of Shechem and Peniel were built in the mountainous region of Ephraim (1 Kgs 12:25), and idolatrous centers of worship at Bethel and Dan were established as direct competitors with Jerusalem and the temple cult there (1 Kgs 12:26–33).[17] Jeroboam's successors continued to build cities such as Samaria and Jericho, all of which represented their rebellion and functioned as anti-Jerusalems (1 Kgs 16:24, 34). After Israel was carried into captivity and the land was resettled with foreigners, they built new cities where they made sacrifices to their gods (2 Kgs 17:29–33).

Apostasy; inter-marriage

The southern kingdom was constantly drawn away from following the LORD, and the majority of its kings were evil.[18] Although there was something of a revival after the fall of the northern kingdom,

16. For the parallels between Jeroboam and the golden calf episode, cf. Frisch, "Exodus Motif," 16–17.

17. Notice the repeated refrain throughout 1–2 Kgs that places the blame at the feet of Israel's first king, Jeroboam: "Jeroboam the son of Nebat, which he made Israel to sin" (e.g., 2 Kgs 10:29; cf. 17:21–31).

18. Of Judah's twenty kings, only eight were righteous in God's eyes: Asa, Jehoshaphat, Joash, Amaziah, Azariah (Uzziah), Jotham, Hezekiah, and Josiah.

by the end of the southern kingdom's existence they had become as wicked as the northern kingdom (Jer 3:6–10; Ezek 23:11–21). Judah had been unfaithful to the Lord and was called a whore on several occasions (e.g., Isa 1:21; Jer 2:20; Ezek 16:15–17).[19] As Cain had built the city of Enoch as a type of anti-Eden, both kingdoms built altars and shrines on the high places that functioned as spiritual anti-Jerusalems (e.g., 1 Kgs 11:6–8; 2 Kgs 17:9–12; Jer 19:4–5;).[20] Like the antediluvians, the land was filled with bloodshed (2 Kgs 21:16; 24:3–4; cf. Ezek 9:9). According to Isaiah, the most fitting city name for the land's inhabitants was not Jerusalem and Judah, but rather Sodom and Gomorrah (Isa 1:10). Instead of yielding the sweet grapes of justice and righteousness, the people had yielded the wild grapes of bloodshed and outcry (Isa 5:3–4, 7).

Prophet/preacher of righteousness

As various authors have noted, the Omride dynasty forms the chiastic centerpiece of the book of Kings, with the ministries of Elijah and Elisha taking center stage.[21] Thus, from a structural analysis of Kings, the conflict between God's word as spoken through Elijah and Elisha and the wicked northern kingdom is the hermeneutical key for interpreting the book as a whole. In addition, God sent many other prophets, some of whose writings form part of the Hebrew Scriptures (cf. Neh 9:30). As for the southern kingdom, God appointed Jeremiah over nations and kingdoms with a similar authority that he had given to those with whom he had made his covenants. However, instead of commanding him to fill the earth with God's glory, he was commanded to uproot, tear down, destroy, and overthrow (Jer 1:10).[22]

19. Ezekiel goes so far as to describe Judah as Sodom's sister (Ezek 16:48-49, 56; 23:31, 33; cf. Jer 23:14).

20. Jeremiah 7:30 and 32:34 say that the temple in Jerusalem itself had been infiltrated.

21. For example, Dorsey, *Literary Structure*, 142–43; Waltke, *Old Testament Theology*, 704.

22. Two other verbs are used —to build and plant (Jer 1:10)—, but the emphasis falls heavily on the destructive side of things.

Affliction; 'crying out'

Similar to how the Egyptians had afflicted the Israelites by placing burdens on them while they were making Pithom and Rameses, Solomon placed burdens on the Israelites to fulfill his construction projects in and around Jerusalem (1 Kgs 11:28; cf. Exod 1:11).[23] Prophets like Jeremiah 'cry out' because of the affliction and violence in the land (e.g., Jer 20:8).

5. Judgment

Near the end of the southern kingdom's existence, its most wicked king, Manasseh, ruled for fifty-five years (2 Kgs 21:1). He filled Jerusalem with very much innocent blood (2 Kgs 21:16; 24:3–4; cf. Ezek 9:9), thereby evoking the horrendous situation just before the flood when man's only thought was to do evil continually, and violence filled the earth (Gen 6:5, 13).

Chaos; flood

It should be no wonder, therefore, that the prophets used flood and chaos imagery to convey God's judgment on Judah.[24] The glory of the LORD, manifested in the form of a cloud that once had filled the temple, has been taken away (Ezek 8–10). Indeed, the temple itself was destroyed and the city's walls were knocked down (2 Kgs 25:1–17). As the LORD had rejected Saul, he now rejects all of Israel's descendants (2 Kgs 17:18–23) and even Jerusalem itself (2 Kgs 23:27). As the earth had been 'formless' and 'void' in the beginning, so too did the LORD make Judah 'formless' and 'void' (Jer 4:23–26).[25] It seems as if God had renounced

23. It is ironic to note that the individual that Solomon placed in charge of these 'burdens' was Jeroboam, the future king of the northern ten tribes of Israel (1 Kgs 11:26–40).

24. Isaiah 24:1–3, 18-20; Jer 4:23–28; Zeph 1:2–6. Flood language is also used to convey the northern kingdom's invasion by the Assyrians (Isa 8:7-8; 17:12-13; Amos 8:8; 9:5). Also, God sent similar plagues to the northern kingdom as he had sent to Egypt (Amos 4:8).

25. For the many parallels between Gen 1 and Jer 4:23–26, cf. Fishbane,

the covenant he made with David (Ps 89:37–51). God has torn down his ordered vineyard and allowed chaos to overcome it (Isa 5:5–6). At the Day of the LORD, invading armies will turn Edenic Jerusalem into a waste wilderness (Joel 2:3).

Exile; expulsion

Already during Solomon's reign, Israel was threatened with being 'sent' from the land if they would forsake God (1 Kgs 9:6–7), as Adam and Eve had been 'sent' from the garden (Gen 3:23). It was due to Manasseh's sins that the southern kingdom went into exile,[26] the story of which is recounted in 2 Kings 23:26–25:26 (esp. 25:21).[27] God has removed Judah —even Jerusalem itself— as he had removed Israel (2 Kgs 23:27). Some fled to Egypt while most others were taken captive to Babylon (2 Kgs 24:1–25:21, 26). Instead of Israel possessing the land from the Nile to the Euphrates, it is Babylon, the emblematic kingdom of chaos, that does so (2 Kgs 24:7). It was during Israel's exile that her imprecatory psalms reached their climax in praying for their enemies's babies —i.e., the Edomites— to be dashed against the rock (Ps 137).

Deliverance of righteous remnant

While it is true that Amos went so far as to imply the destruction of even the remnant of Israel (Amos 9:1–4), this must be qualified by his other statements that a remnant would indeed survive (Amos 5:3; 6:9–10). His point, however, was to be taken seriously: God's anger was such that it would appear as if he would completely annihilate Israel, and even the small surviving remnant would be meaningless to the survival of the nation as a whole.[28]

"Jeremiah *IV* 23-26"; Craigie et al., *Jeremiah 1–25*, 81. Interestingly, this judgment of exile also forms an *inclusio* with the beginning of the Abraham cycle: Abraham was taken out of Babylon and his descendants were ultimately exiled back there; cf. Messmer, "Possible Chiastic Center."

26. Second Kgs 23:26–27; 24:3–4; Jer 15:4; Ezek 12:19.

27. For the story of the northern kingdom's exile, cf. 2 Kgs 17:6–23.

28. Hasel, *The Remnant*, 392.

Many Jews would be killed by the flood waters of the Assyrian and Babylonian armies, and yet God preserved a remnant for himself.[29] In fact, in a stunning act of reversal, Isaiah 13–14 predicted the downfall of Babylon like that of Sodom and Gomorrah, and that God would once again make Israel 'rest' in her land (Isa 14:1–3).[30]

Elijah and Elisha

The seventh king of Israel was Ahab, and the tenth Jehu, who were the primary kings that Elijah and Elisha interacted with, respectively.[31] Ahab was arguably the worst northern king and Jehu was anointed by Elisha to bring judgment on the Omride dynasty. Thus, it is tempting to see Elijah as inaugurating judgment on Israel and Elisha as inaugurating a new creation. This idea is further enhanced when it is recognized that Elijah is being cast as a second Moses.[32] However, the author of Kings has not provided a complete cycle of creation, man, fall, division, and judgment, which is why it has not been included in the primary text above.

Uzziah

The tenth ruler over Judah, the southern kingdom, was Uzziah/Azariah (2 Kgs 15:13).[33] Uzziah was the first godly king after the

29. Second Kgs 19:30–31; Isa 10:22–23; Jer 24:4–10; 29:10–14.

30. There is a clear play on the theme of 'rest' in Isa 13:20–14:4, which employs four different Hebrew words that are used six times altogether; cf. Wegner, *A Student's Guide*, 166 n. 42.

31. These numbers hold if Tibni is not counted as a king. It does not appear that he reigned, or if he did, it was insignificant (1 Kgs 16:21–22).

32. Cf. Allison, *New Moses*, 39–45. Trompf writes, "Of all the prophets, Elijah is the one most strikingly presented as a new Moses" ("Notions of Historical Recurrence," 215).

33. The figure depends on how one calculates the kings, and whether or not one includes Queen Athaliah in the list. If one reckons from David, begins the start of the count with Solomon, and does not include Athaliah, then Uzziah is the tenth king after David. If one reckons from Solomon, begins the start of the count with Solomon, and does not include Athaliah, then there are

Jehu-dominated kings Ahaziah, Athaliah (actually a queen), Jehoash, and Amaziah. God's chosen people continue to reduce, as does their geographical sphere of influence.

1. Creation

Creation from chaos

Uzziah's father, Amaziah, worshipped the Edomite gods (2 Chr 25:14) and foolishly challenged Joash, king of Israel, to battle, which he lost (2 Chr 25:17ff.). This was done as God's retribution on Amaziah for his idolatry (2 Chr 25:20). Because of the loss, Jerusalem's walls were broken down, the temple was ransacked, and Jerusalem was impoverished (2 Chr 25:23–24). In the end, Amaziah was murdered by his own people at the instigation of the Lord (2 Chr 25:27).

Creation battle

Eloth/Elath was restored to Judah (2 Chr 26:2) and Uzziah defeated the Philistines, Arabians, and Ammonites (2 Chr 26:6–8).

2. Man

Election

Aside from wicked Manasseh, Uzziah enjoyed the longest reign of the Judean kings: 52 years (2 Kgs 15:2; 2 Chr 26:3). He did what was right in God's eyes, in large part thanks to Zechariah (2 Chr 26:4–5).[34]

---

ten kings from Solomon to Uzziah. If one reckons from Solomon, begins the start of the count with Rehoboam, and does include Athaliah, then Uzziah is the tenth king to rule over the southern kingdom.

34. Possibly the same Zechariah mentioned in Isa 8:2.

Mixed multitude

Nevertheless, Uzziah did not remove the high places from the land, and the people continued to sacrifice to foreign gods (2 Kgs 15:4).

Mountain and garden

Uzziah built towers in the wilderness, hewed cisterns, had large herds, and employed farmers and vinedressers in the hills (2 Chr 26:10), all of which can be seen to evoke Edenic imagery.

Divine blessing and commands

Uzziah in the south, combined with Jeroboam II in the north, briefly restored Israel's two kingdoms to approximately the same boundaries as they were under Solomon, and the important seaport Elath/Eloth was recaptured, a feat only recorded to have been accomplished by Solomon (1 Kgs 9:26–28; 1 Chr 8:17–18). Uzziah's fame spread far, and his fame was connected to his strength (2 Chr 26:8, 15).

3. Fall[35]

Not vigilant

Upon growing strong, Uzziah became proud (2 Chr 26:16). This pride replaced his earlier seeking of God and following the instruction of Zechariah (2 Chr 26:5). He has ceased fearing the LORD.

Woman; deception/seduction; usurpation

By his own hubris, Uzziah attempted to usurp the role that was reserved for the priests alone.[36] His pursuit of "honor" had seduced

35. Morgenstern, "Amos Studies II," Begg, "Uzziah (Azariah) of Judah," Stordalen, *Echoes of Eden*, 446–47 ("Taking the law into his own hands, Uzziah replays the role of Adam"). Cf. *Targum of Isaiah* 28:21a for the same tradition.

36. Josephus adds interesting details to this account, one of which is that the feast was the Day of Atonement (*Antiq.* 9.222–27). In this reading, Uzziah was usurping the right to burn incense on the incense altar during Judah's

him to think that God's established laws did not apply to him (2 Chr 26:18).[37]

Knowledge of sin

Uzziah was stricken with leprosy. The priests immediately recognized what had happened and rushed Uzziah out of the temple (2 Chr 26:19–20). Apparently Uzziah needed no convincing of his guilt, as he put up no resistance. His removal from the temple mirrors Adam and Eve's removal from the garden of Eden.

Curse

Uzziah was a leper for the rest of his life and lived in a separate house (2 Chr 26:21).

Forgiveness

Nevertheless, Uzziah was buried with his fathers (2 Chr 26:22–23).

4. Division

This is where the pattern of the cycles appears to stop.

---

most important and holy feast day.

37. In Ezek 31:18, "honor" (translated as "glory"; Heb: כָּבוֹד) is connected with Eden.

Appendix IV: Regular Spacing between the Cycles

The careful reader of this work probably will have noticed that the introduction to each cycle begins with a temporal marker, either a relative genealogical marker or a chronological approximation. This information was not introduced as a major theme because there does not seem to be clearly-established pattern that would justify it. Nevertheless, enough of a pattern does exist to justify some exploratory comments in an appendix. In brief, I am suggesting that the cycles exhibit a stable spacing of approximately ten generations or four- to five-hundred years.[1]

For at least five of the cycles there is a consistent spacing of ten generations between them. The first three cycles are rather straightforward whereas the subsequent two require a bit more explanation. Regarding the first two cycles, a simple reading of the text demonstrates that there are ten generations between Adam and Noah (Gen 5),[2] and another ten generations between Noah and Abraham (Gen 11:10–26). At the very least, this ten-generation pattern suggests that at least some of the biblical cycles are well-ordered, predictable, and controlled by a sovereign God.[3]

1. For the importance of the number ten, cf. Origen, *Comm. John* 10:1.
2. In the Sumerian King List, there are also ten antediluvian kings.
3. It should be noted that this is not a novel way of reading the biblical

As for the third cycle, the evidence is ambiguous as the spacing can be calculated to either ten or fifteen generations between Abraham and the generation that entered the Promised Land under Joshua. As for the ten-generation option, according to the genealogies presented in the Pentateuch, Moses is the seventh generation from Abraham,[4] which would make his younger contemporary, Joshua, part of the eighth. Joshua's generation died in the desert (Num 14:26–35), and the ninth wandered in the desert for forty years (Num 32:13). This means that it was the tenth generation —when Moses was 120 years old (Deut 31:2; 34:7)— that entered the Promised Land (Num 14:31).[5]

As for the fifteen-generation option, according to the genealogy provided in 1 Chronicles 7:20–27, Joshua is the tenth descendant from Ephraim, making him part of the thirteenth generation from Abraham. Factoring in the two generations of the wilderness previously mentioned, one arrives at fifteen generations. According to traditional chronological reckonings, Abraham was born in the twenty-second century BC and Joshua was born sometime either in the fifteenth century BC (early Exodus date) or in the thirteenth century BC (late Exodus date), thus opening up a gap of between 700 and 900 years between the two.

---

story. For Jewish sources, cf. m. Avot 5:2; *ARN*, 32–33; for a Christian source, cf. Irenaeus, *Demonstration*, 11–24. Many ancient sources specifically mention the ten-generation scheme. The reference to ten generations in Deut 23:2–3 seems to evoke the idea of perpetuity, but the fact that eunuchs are readmitted to the people of God in Isa 56:3–5 makes the idea of perpetuity uncertain. Also, according to lunar reckoning, a woman's gestation period lasts ten months. This may suggest a connection between the two with regard to life cycles.

4. Exodus 6:16–20; Num 26.57–59; cf. 1 Chr 23:6–13. Jack Sasson has provocatively suggested: "It may be highly coincidental that Moses's generation, the 26th since Creation, is equivalent to the gematria of the tetra-grammaton (Y = 10; H = 5; W = 6; H = 5)" ("The 'Tower of Babel,'" 214 n. 7; "A Genealogical 'Convention,'" 12 n. 2).

5. Assuming forty years to a generation, perhaps this explains Gen 15:13 where God tells Abraham that his descendants would be "sojourners in a land that is not theirs and will be servants there, and they will be afflicted for four hundred years."

As for the fourth cycle between Moses–Joshua and David, the time between the Exodus and the building of the temple is identified in 1 Kings 6:1 as spanning 480 years. If a generation roughly spanned forty years, then this would suggest twelve generations between the two events. However, this figure can be reduced from 480 years to 400, thereby implying ten generations. The Exodus generation wandered in the wilderness for forty years and died there, thereby reducing the figure to 440 years. Also, it was David's successor, Solomon, who began building the temple, thereby necessitating the reduction of another generation, which not unreasonably can be taken as forty years.[6] This means that approximately 400 years separate the Moses/Joshua cycle from the David cycle, which not unreasonably can be taken to equal ten generations.[7]

As for the fifth and sixth cycles, while there does not appear to be a way to confirm how many generations stand between them, a few interesting observations can be noted.[8] Regarding the cycle from David to the Babylonian captivity, an interesting coincidence with 2 Samuel 11–12 (David's affair with Bathsheba and murder of Uriah) suggests itself as an important date, again under the assumption that forty years is equivalent to a generation. Being that the southern kingdom ended in 586 BC, 400 years earlier would be 986 BC, or the twenty-fourth year of David's reign (himself being about fifty-five years old). Leaving this date aside for the moment, it is now important to calculate Solomon's birth. Since there is no birth date given with respect to anyone else, the next best option available is his ascension date. The sources do not concur

6. The evidence is difficult to interpret since no text explicitly says how long a generation lasts. Numbers 32:13; Deut 2:14; Ps 95:10 connect forty years with a generation, but they are also talking about the generation that wandered in the wilderness, which could be a special case.

7. Interestingly, however, David can also be considered the tenth generation from Perez, son of Judah (1 Chr 2:5, 9–17; Ruth 4:18–22). This, in turn, would make him the fourteenth generation from Abraham, which corresponds to Matthew's genealogy (Matt 1:2–6).

8. Matthew 1 puts twenty-eight generations between David and Jesus, and Luke 3 puts forty-two.

exactly but a general idea does emerge: the LXX reading of 1 Kings 2:12 and Eupolemus (34:20) say that Solomon was twelve years old when he began to rule, Josephus says he was fourteen (*Antiq* 8:211), 1 Chronicles 22:5 and 29:1 say that he was "young" without specifying his age, and in 1 Kings 3:7 Solomon calls himself a "little child" again without specifying his age.[9] Thus assuming that he was about twelve years old at his ascension to the throne, this would mean that he was born in c. 982 BC. When it is remembered that Solomon was the child of David and Bathsheba (2 Sam 12:24), and that there was some time between the Uriah incident and the birth of Solomon (2 Sam 12:24),[10] we arrive at the conclusion that almost 400 years exactly separates David's sin with Bathsheba and the fall of Jerusalem in 586 BC. If, as was argued above, forty years represents a generation, then ten generations also separate David from the exile generation.[11]

Regarding the last cycle from the Babylonian captivity to Jesus Christ, Daniel 9:24–27 was used by Jews as the fundamental text associated with calculating the coming of the Messiah, and that the calculation hovers around 400–500 years, again evoking the ten-generation scheme.

9. According to this reading, Solomon would have fathered his son Rehoboam when he was just thirteen years old, since he had a forty-one-year-old son after he had reigned for forty years (1 Kgs 11:42; 14:21). While this may seem incredible to modern sensibilities, it was not so to ancient ones, especially when the person under consideration was the king.

10. If the entirety of 2 Sam 11–12 is to be read in chronological order, then the time would have been less than the time it took to siege Rabbah (2 Sam 11:1; 12:26).

11. Otherwise, it is also interesting to note that during the divided monarchy period (i.e., post-Solomon until the exiles), each kingdom had twenty kings, therefore totaling forty kings in all. This number may have symbolic value as a complete generation of kings during this cycle.

Bibliography

Allison, Dale. *The New Moses: A Matthean Typology*. Eugene, OR: Wipf and Stock, 1993.

Athas, George. "The Creation of Israel: The cosmic Proportions of the Exodus Event." In *Exploring Exodus: Literary, Theological and Contemporary Approaches*, edited by Brian Rosner and Paul Williamson. Downers Grove, IL: InterVarsity, 2008.

Beale, G. K. *The Temple and the Church's Mission: A Biblical Theology of the Dwelling Place of God*. New Studies in Biblical Theology 17. Downers Grove, IL: InterVarsity, 2004.

Begg, Christopher. "Uzziah (Azariah) of Judah According to Josephus." *EB* 53 no 1 (1995) 5–24.

Beitzel, Barry. *The Moody Atlas of Bible Lands*. Chicago: Moody, 1985.

Bergsma, John, and Scott Hahn. "Noah's Nakedness and the Curse on Canaan (Genesis 9:20–27)." *JBL* 124 no 1 (2005) 25–40.

Block, Daniel. *Judges, Ruth: An Exegetical and Theological Exposition of Holy Scripture*. New American Commentary 6. Nashville, TN: Broadman & Holman, 1999.

Bodi, Daniel. *The Book of Ezekiel and the Poem of Erra*. Göttingen: Vandenhoeck & Ruprecht, 1991.

Brown, John Pairman. "The Mediterranean vocabulary of the vine." *VT* 19 (1969) 146–70.

Budd, Philip. *Numbers*. Word Biblical Commentary 5. Waco, TX: Word Books, 1984.

Butler, Trent. *Joshua 13–24*, 2nd ed. Word Biblical Commentary 7B. Grand Rapids: Zondervan, 2014.

———. *Judges*. Word Biblical Commentary 8. Nashville, TN: Thomas Nelson, 2009.

Campbell, Anthony. *The Ark Narrative (1 Sam 4–6; 2 Sam 6): A Form-Critical and Traditio-Historical Study*. SBL Dissertation Series 16. Missoula, MT: Scholars' Press, 1975.

Carmichael, Calum. *The Sacrificial Laws of Leviticus and the Joseph Story*. Cambridge: Cambridge University Press, 2017.

Cassuto, Umberto. *A Commentary on the Book of Exodus*. Jerusalem: Magnes, 1967.

Childs, Brevard. "The Enemy from the North and the Chaos Tradition." *JBL* 78 no 3 (1959) 187–98.

Clines, David. *The Theme of the Pentateuch*. Journal for the Study of the Old Testament Supplement Series 10. Sheffield: Sheffield Academic Press, 1992.

Condie, Keith. "Narrative Features of Numbers 13–14 and their significance for the Meaning of the Book of Numbers." *RTR* 60 no 3 (2001) 123–37.

Craigie, Peter, Page Kelley, and Joel Drinkard. *Jeremiah 1–25*. Word Biblical Commentary 26. Dallas, TX: Word Books, 1991.

Cresson, Bruce. "The condemnation of Edom in Postexilic Judaism." In *The Use of the Old Testament in the New and Other Essays: Studies in Honor of William Franklin Stinespring*, edited by James Efird, 125–148. Durham, NC: Duke University Press, 1972.

Cullmann, Oscar. *Christ and Time: The Primitive Christian Conception of Time and History*, 3rd edition. Translated by Floyd Filson. Eugene, OR: Wipf & Stock, 1962.

Daube, David. *The Exodus Pattern in the Bible*. London: Faber and Faber, 1963.

Davies, John. "'Discerning Between Good and Evil': Solomon as a New Adam in 1 Kings." *WTJ* 73 (2011) 39–57.

DelHousaye, John. *The Fourfold Gospel: A Formational Commentary on Matthew, Mark, Luke, and John*, volume 1. Eugene, OR: Pickwick, 2020.

Dicou, Bert. *Edom, Israel's Brother and Antagonist: The Role of Edom in Biblical Prophecy and Story*. Sheffield: Sheffield Academic Press, 1994.

Dorsey, David. *The Literary Structure of the Old Testament: A Commentary on Genesis–Malachi*. Grand Rapids: Baker Academic, 1999.

Dunphy, Graeme. "Six Ages of the World." In *Encyclopedia of the Medieval Chronicle*, edited by Graeme Dunphy., 1367–70. Leiden: Brill, 2010).

Ellul, Jacques. *The Meaning of the City*. Grand Rapids: Eerdmans, 1970.

Fishbane, Michael. "Jeremiah *IV* 23-26 and Job *III* 3-13." *VT* 21 (1971) 151–67.

Freitheim, Terrence. *Exodus*. Louisville, KY: John Knox, 1991.

Frisch, Amos. "The Exodus Motif in 1 Kings 1–14." *JSOT* 87 (2000) 3–21.

Gage, Warren. *The Gospel of Genesis: Studies in Protology and Eschatology*. Eugene, OR: Wipf & Stock, 1984.

Gordon, Robert. *Holy Land, Holy City: Sacred Geography and the Interpretation of the Bible*. Carlisle, UK: Paternoster, 2004.

Hasel, Gerhard. *Old Testament Theology: Basic Issues in the Current Debate*, 4th edition. Grand Rapids: Eerdmans, 1991.

———. *The Remnant: The History and Theology of the Remnant Idea from Genesis to Isaiah*. Berrien Springs, MI: Andrews University Press, 1972.

Hilhorst, Anthony. "Ager Damascenus: Views on the Place of Adam's Creation." *WST* 20 no 2 (2007) 131–44.

Hinckley, Robert. "Adam, Aaron, and the Garden Sanctuary." *Logia* 22 no 4 (2013) 5–12.

Kearney, Peter. "Creation and Liturgy: The P Redaction of Ex 25–40." *ZAW* 89 (1977) 375–387.

Keel, Othmar. *The Symbolism of the Biblical World: Ancient Near Eastern Iconography and the Book of Psalms.* Translated by Timothy Hallett. New York: Seabury, 1978.

Kim, Koowon. "Eli, 'Enemy of a Temple'? A Study of מעון in 1 Samuel 2.29 and 2.32." *BT* 70 no 1 (2019) 50–63.

Klein, Ralph. *1 Samuel.* Word Biblical Commentary 10. Nashville, TN: Thomas Nelson, 2000.

Lawson, John. *The Biblical Theology of Saint Irenaeus.* London: Epworth, 1948.

Link Jr., Peter, and Matthew Emerson. "Searching for the Second Adam: Typological Connections between Adam, Joseph, Mordecai, and Daniel." *SBJT* 21 no 1 (2017) 123–44.

Long, Burke. "A Darkness between Brothers: Solomon and Adonijah." *JSOT* 19 (1981) 79–94.

Marlowe, W. Creighton. "The Sin of Shinar (Genesis 11:4)." *EJT* 20 no 1 (2011) 29–39.

Marshall, I. Howard. *Commentary on Luke.* Exeter: The Paternoster Press, 1978.

Matthews, Kenneth. *Genesis 1–11:26.* New American Commentary 1A. Nashville: Broadman & Holman, 1996.

Messmer, Andrew. "A Possible Chiastic Center for Primary History (Genesis–2 Kings)." *VT* 69 no 2 (2019) 232–40.

Miller, J. Maxwell, and John Hayes, *A History of Ancient Israel and Judah*, 2nd edition. Louisville, KY: Westminster John Knox, 2006.

Morales, Michael. *Exodus Old and New: A Biblical Theology of Redemption.* Downers Grove, IL: InterVarsity, 2020.

Morgenstern, Julian. "Amos Studies II: The Sin of Uzziah, the Festival of Jeroboam and the Date of Amos." *HUCA* 12–13 (1937–1938) 1–53.

Nolland, John. *Luke.* Word Biblical Commentary 35A. Nashville, TN: Thomas Nelson, 1989.

O'Connell, Robert. *The Rhetoric of the Book of Judges.* Brill: Leiden, 1996.

Olson, Dennis. *Numbers.* Louisville, KY: Westminster John Knox, 1996.

Ottosson, Magnus. "Eden and the Land of Promise." In *Congress Volume: Jerusalem 1986*, edited by J. A. Emerton, 177–88. Leiden: Brill, 1988.

Parker, Kim. "Repetition as a Structure Device in 1 Kings 1–11." *JSOT* 42 (1988) 19–27.

Postell, Seth. *Adam as Israel: Genesis 1–3 as the Introduction to the Torah and Tanakh.* Eugene, OR: Pickwick Publications, 2011.

Rendsburg, Gary. *The Redaction of Genesis.* Winona Lake, IN: Eisenbrauns, 1986.

Roberts, Alastair, and Andrew Wilson. *Echoes of Exodus: Tracing Themes of Redemption through Scripture.* Wheaton, IL: Crossway, 2018.

Sailhamer, John. *The Pentateuch as Narrative*. Grand Rapids: Zondervan, 1992.

Sasson, Jack. "A Genealogical 'Convention' in Biblical Chronography?" *ZAW* 90 no 2 (1978) 171–85.

———. "The 'Tower of Babel' as a Clue to the Redactional Structure of the Primeval History [Gen 1-11 9]." In *The Bible World: Essays in Honor of Cyrus H Gordon*, edited by Gordon Rendsburg, et al., 211–19. New York: Ktav, 1980.

Smith, Ralph. *Micah–Malachi*. Word Biblical Commentary 32. Nashville, TN: Thomas Nelson, 1984

Smolar, Leivy, and Moshe Aberbach. "The Golden Calf Episode in Postbiblical Literature." *HUCA* 39 (1968) 91–116.

Stordalen, Terje. *Echoes of Eden: Genesis 2–3 and Symbolism of the Eden Garden in Biblical Hebrew Literature*. Leuven: Peeters, 2000.

Sweeney, Marvin. "Davidic Polemics in the Book of Judges." *VT* 47 no 4 (1997) 517–29.

Tate, Marvin. *Psalms 51–100*. Word Biblical Commentary 20; Nashville, TN: Thomas Nelson, 1990.

Tomasino, Anthony. "History Repeats Itself: The 'Fall' and Noah's Drunkenness." *VT* 42 no 1 (1992) 128–30.

Trompf, G. W. *The Idea of Historical Recurrence in Western Thought: From Antiquity to the Reformation*. Berkley, CA: University of California Press, 1979.

———. "Notions of Historical Recurrence in Classical Hebrew Historiography." In *Studies in the Historical Books of the Old Testament*, edited by J. A. Emerton, 213–29. Leiden: Brill, 1979.

Wacholder, Ben Zion. "Chronomessianism: The Timing of Messianic Movements and the Calendar of Sabbatical Cycles." *HUCA* 46 (1975) 201–18.

Waltke, Bruce. *An Old Testament Theology: an Exegetical, Canonical, and Thematic Approach*. Grand Rapids: Zondervan, 2007.

Waltke, Bruce, with Cathi Fredricks. *Genesis: A Commentary*. Grand Rapids: Zondervan, 2001.

Walton, John. *Genesis 1 as Ancient Cosmology*. Winona Lake, IN: Eisenbrauns, 2011.

Watts, John. *Isaiah 34-66*, revised edition. Word Biblical Commentary 25. Nashville, TN: Thomas Nelson, 2005.

Wegner, Paul. *A Student's Guide to Textual Criticism of the Bible: Its History, Methods & Results*. Downers Grove, IL: IVP Academic, 2006.

Wenham, Gordon. *Genesis 1–15*. Word Biblical Commentary 1. Nashville: Thomas Nelson, 1987.

Williamson, H. G. M. *Ezra and Nehemiah*. Sheffield: JSOT, 1996.

Winnett, Frederick. *The Mosaic Tradition*. Toronto: University of Toronto Press, 1949.

Wright, N. T. *The New Testament and the People of God*. Minneapolis: Fortress, 1992.

www.ingramcontent.com/pod-product-compliance
Lightning Source LLC
LaVergne TN
LVHW050638100826
845148LV00011B/1897